THE SCIENCE OF REVISION

Illustrations and words

Research has shown that revising with words and pictures doubles the quality of responses by students.[1] This is known as 'dual-coding' because it provides two ways of fetching the information from our brain. The improvement in responses is particularly apparent in students when they are asked to apply their knowledge to different problems. Recall, application and judgement are all specifically and carefully assessed in public examination questions.

Retrieval of information

Retrieval practice encourages students to come up with answers to questions.[2] The closer the question is to one you might see in a real examination, the better. Also, the closer the environment in which a student revises is to the 'examination environment', the better. Students who had a test 2–7 days away did 30% better using retrieval practice than students who simply read, or repeatedly reread material. Students who were expected to teach the content to someone else after their revision period did better still.[3] What was found to be most interesting in other studies is that students using retrieval methods and testing for revision were also more resilient to the introduction of stress.[4]

Ebbinghaus' forgetting curve and spaced learning

Ebbinghaus' 140-year-old study examined the rate at which we forget things over time. The findings still hold true. However, the act of forgetting facts and techniques and relearning them is what cements them into the brain.[5] Spacing out revision is more effective than cramming – we know that, but students should also know that the space between revisiting material should vary depending on how far away the examination is. A cyclical approach is required. An examination 12 months away necessitates revisiting covered material about once a month. A test in 30 days should have topics revisited every 3 days – intervals of roughly a tenth of the time available.[6]

Summary

Students: the more tests and past questions you do, in an environment as close to examination conditions as possible, the better you are likely to perform on the day. If you prefer to listen to music while you revise, tunes without lyrics will be far less detrimental to your memory and retention. Silence is most effective.[5] If you choose to study with friends, choose carefully – effort is contagious.[7]

---

1. Mayer, R. E., & Anderson, R. B. (1991). Animations need narrations: An experimental test of dual-coding hypothesis. *Journal of Education Psychology*, (83)4, 484–490.
2. Roediger III, H. L., & Karpicke, J.D. (2006). Test-enhanced learning: Taking memory tests improves long-term retention. *Psychological Science*, 17(3), 249–255.
3. Nestojko, J., Bui, D., Kornell, N. & Bjork, E. (2014). Expecting to teach enhances learning and organisation of knowledge in free recall of text passages. *Memory and Cognition*, 42(7), 1038–1048.
4. Smith, A. M., Floerke, V. A., & Thomas, A. K. (2016) Retrieval practice protects memory against acute stress. *Science*, 354(6315), 1046–1048.
5. Perham, N., & Currie, H. (2014). Does listening to preferred music improve comprehension performance? *Applied Cognitive Psychology*, 28(2), 279–284.
6. Cepeda, N. J., Vul, E., Rohrer, D., Wixted, J. T. & Pashler, H. (2008). Spacing effects in learning a temporal ridgeline of optimal retention. *Psychological Science*, 19(11), 1095–1102.
7. Busch, B. & Watson, E. (2019), *The Science of Learning*, 1st ed. Routledge.

CONTENTS

Assessment objectives vi

Exam technique

The poetry anthology exam question 2
Structuring your answer 3
Planning your answer 4
Writing your answer 5
Technical accuracy 8
Checking your answer 9

Analysis of poems

When We Two Parted — Lord Byron 10
    Comparing *When We Two Parted* 16
Love's Philosophy — Percy Bysshe Shelley 18
    Comparing *Love's Philosophy* 24
Porphyria's Lover — Robert Browning 26
    Comparing *Porphyria's Lover* 32
Sonnet 29 — 'I think of thee!' — Elizabeth Barrett Browning 34
    Comparing *Sonnet 29 — 'I think of thee!'* 40
Neutral Tones — Thomas Hardy 42
    Comparing *Neutral Tones* 48
The Farmer's Bride — Charlotte Mew 50
    Comparing *The Farmer's Bride* 56
Walking Away — Cecil Day-Lewis 58
    Comparing *Walking Away* 64
Letters from Yorkshire — Maura Dooley 66
    Comparing *Letters from Yorkshire* 72
Eden Rock — Charles Causley 74
    Comparing *Eden Rock* 80
Follower — Seamus Heaney 82
    Comparing *Follower* 88
Mother, Any Distance — Simon Armitage 90
    Comparing *Mother, Any Distance* 96
Before You Were Mine — Carol Ann Duffy 98
    Comparing *Before You Were Mine* 104

Winter Swans — Owen Sheers .... 106 ☐
    Comparing *Winter Swans* .... 112 ☐
Singh Song! — Daljit Nagra .... 114 ☐
    Comparing *Singh Song!* .... 120 ☐
Climbing My Grandfather — Andrew Waterhouse .... 122 ☐
    Comparing *Climbing My Grandfather* .... 128 ☐
Overview of themes .... 130 ☐
Examination practice .... 131 ☐

Examination practice answers .... 132 ☐
Levels-based mark schemes for extended response questions .... 134 ☐
Index .... 135 ☐
Examination tips .... 137 ☐

MARK ALLOCATIONS

All the questions in this book require extended responses. These answers should be marked as a whole in accordance with the levels of response guidance on **page 134**. The answers provided are examples only. There are many more points to make than there are marks available, so the answers are not exhaustive.

ASSESSMENT OBJECTIVES

In the exam, your answer will be marked against assessment objectives (AOs). It's important you understand which skills each AO tests.

AO1

- Show the ability to read, understand and respond to texts.
- Answers should maintain a critical style and develop an informed personal response.
- Use examples from the text, including quotes, to support and illustrate points.

AO2

- Analyse the language, form and structure used by a writer to create meanings and effects, using relevant subject terminology where appropriate.

AO3

- Show understanding of the relationships between texts and the contexts in which they were written.

The AOs on this page have been written in simple language. See the AQA website for the official wording.

There are 12 marks available for AO1, 12 marks for AO2 and 6 marks for AO3.

PAPER 2
Modern texts and poetry

Information about Paper 2

Written exam: 2 hours 15 minutes (this includes the questions on modern texts and unseen poetry)

96 marks (30 marks for modern texts plus 4 marks for SPaG, 30 marks for the poetry anthology and 32 marks for unseen poetry)

60% of the qualification grade (20% for modern texts, 20% for the poetry anthology and 20% for unseen poetry)

This guide covers the section on the Love and Relationships poetry anthology.

Questions
One extended-writing question on a modern text (you will be given a choice of two questions, but you should only answer one), one extended-writing question on the poetry anthology you have studied and two questions on the unseen poems.

THE POETRY ANTHOLOGY EXAM QUESTION

The poetry anthology is tested in Paper 2, along with a question on a modern text you have studied and two questions on unseen poems.

Example question

Here's an example exam-style question for the Love and Relationships poetry anthology:

> Compare how poets present ideas about the power of love in *Sonnet 29 — 'I think of thee!'* and **one** other poem from Love and Relationships. [30 marks]

How to answer the question

- There will only be one question per anthology: you won't be given a choice of questions.
- You will need to compare the poem specified in the question with one other poem from the Love and Relationships anthology. It's up to you which poem you choose.
- Don't write about more than one poem in addition to the printed poem. You won't get any extra marks.
- The poem specified in the question will be printed in full. Although you will be given a list of the poems from the anthology, the other poems will not be printed out and you're not allowed to take notes into the exam with you.
- The question will specify a theme. In the example above, the theme is 'the power of love', but the theme could be anything related to the poems in the cluster: romantic love, heartbreak, family relationships etc. We've summarised some of the main themes shared across the cluster on **page 130**.
- You will need to write an essay-style response to the question.
- It's not enough to point out techniques used by the poets. You need to comment on their effect on you as the reader, and link them back to the theme.
- This question is worth 30 marks. You should spend about 45 minutes on the question. This includes planning and checking time.

Your exam paper will also include questions on the **Power and Conflict** and **Worlds and Lives** anthologies.

Do not answer questions about poems you have not studied.

STRUCTURING YOUR ANSWER

Most poems can be interpreted in several different ways, and any interpretation is valid as long as you can support your answer with sensible evidence from the poem or the poem's context.

Choosing a poem

In the exam, you will need to decide which poem to compare with the poem given in the question. You should pick a poem which will give you plenty to write about. The poems don't have to share similarities; you can talk about the poems' differences too.

All the poems in the cluster are linked, but some can be compared more effectively than others. When you're revising, you could group poems together by theme, so you can quickly choose a suitable poem in the exam. (Take a look at our handy table on **page 130** to help you.)

We've highlighted some common themes that can be found across the cluster, such as romantic love, family relationships, distance and heartbreak but these themes aren't exhaustive: there are lots more ways that poems can be thematically linked.

Structuring your answer

There are two main ways you can structure your exam answer.

Option one

You could analyse one aspect of a poem (i.e. a point about language, form, structure or context), and then directly compare how the second poem is similar or different.

Practise answering exam-style questions to see which structure works best for you.

Option two

You could write several paragraphs about the first poem, and then several paragraphs about the second poem.

Whichever structure you choose, make sure your response answers the question.

GCSE English Literature Poetry Anthology | Love and Relationships

PLANNING YOUR ANSWER

You should spend about five minutes on a plan, but make sure you're happy with your plan before you start writing.

Plan

It's helpful to jot down a plan before you start writing. This will help make sure that you have enough to write about, and that your answer stays on-track. Think about the comparisons you can make across the poems' content, theme, language, form and structure. You must include details about the poems' context to get full marks.

Your plan could be a spider diagram, a table or just some notes. Use whichever technique you prefer.

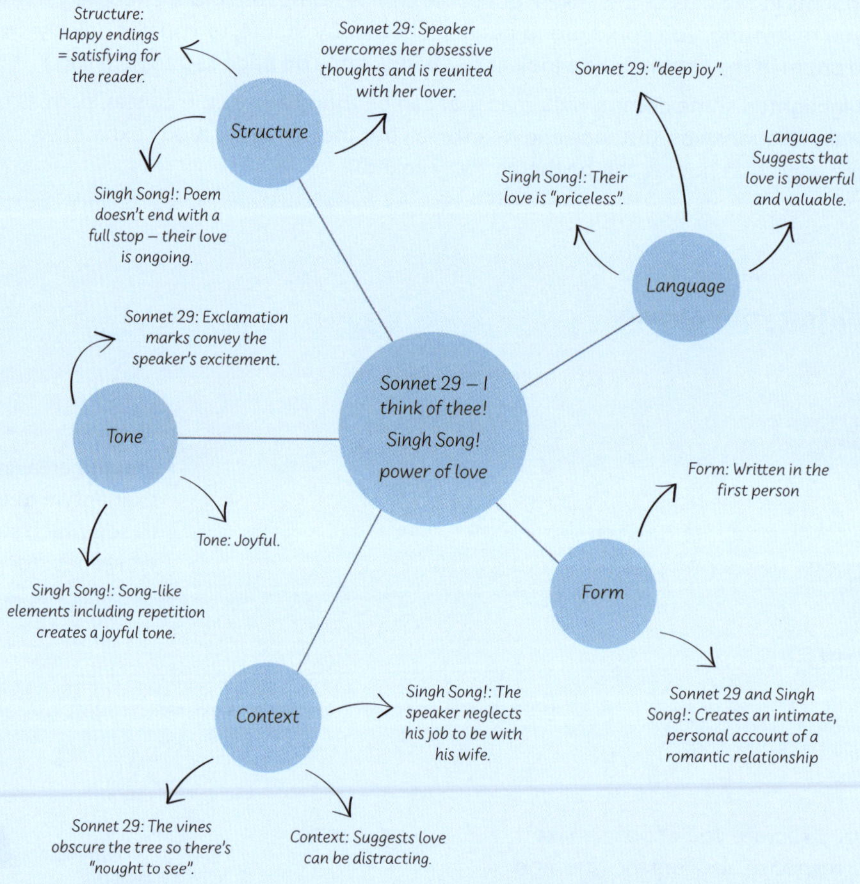

Here's an example plan for the question on **page 2**.

Structure: Happy endings = satisfying for the reader.

Sonnet 29: Speaker overcomes her obsessive thoughts and is reunited with her lover.

Sonnet 29: "deep joy".

Structure

Singh Song!: Poem doesn't end with a full stop – their love is ongoing.

Singh Song!: Their love is "priceless".

Language: Suggests that love is powerful and valuable.

Language

Sonnet 29: Exclamation marks convey the speaker's excitement.

Tone

Sonnet 29 – I think of thee! Singh Song! power of love

Form: Written in the first person

Form

Tone: Joyful.

Singh Song!: Song-like elements including repetition creates a joyful tone.

Context

Singh Song!: The speaker neglects his job to be with his wife.

Sonnet 29 and Singh Song!: Creates an intimate, personal account of a romantic relationship

Sonnet 29: The vines obscure the tree so there's "nought to see".

Context: Suggests love can be distracting.

If you're struggling to plan an answer with the poem you've picked, try writing a new plan with a different poem. It's better to spend an extra 5 minutes on another plan than committing to a pair of poems which don't fully answer the question.

WRITING YOUR ANSWER

You should spend about 35 minutes writing your answer.

Introduction

A good introduction should briefly introduce which two poems you are comparing and how they both link to the theme specified in the question. For example:

Example

'Sonnet 29 — 'I think of thee!'' and 'Singh Song!' explore the power of romantic love. 'Sonnet 29 — 'I think of thee!'' focuses on a speaker who is overcome with thoughts of her lover, whereas 'Singh Song!' examines the relationship of a newly married couple. Both speakers suggest that love is joyful, but they also present it as overwhelming and distracting.

Main answer

The main part of your answer should compare 3–4 of the following:

- **Form:** What type of poem is it (i.e. sonnet, dramatic monologue)? Does it have a rhyme scheme or is it written in free verse? Whose perspective is the poem told from?
- **Content:** What happens in the poem?
- **Structure:** How many stanzas are there? How are the events ordered and revealed to the reader? Are any lines repeated?
- **Syntax:** How have the lines been constructed? Is there caesura (a deliberate pause in a line), enjambment (when a sentence runs on to the next line), or end-stopping (when a line finishes with the end of a sentence)? Have words been deliberately placed at the start of a line for emphasis?
- **Tone:** What feelings are conveyed by the poem?
- **Language:** What language techniques has the poet used (i.e. alliteration, similes, sensory language)?
- **Theme:** What's the deeper meaning of the poem?
- **Message:** Is the poet trying to tell the reader something?
- **Context:** What was happening at the time the poet was writing which may have influenced the poem?

For every feature you write about, you need to:
- Explain how it answers the question.
- Comment on the effect it has on you as the reader.

 You don't need to include examples of all these features. It's far better to write about fewer things in more detail, than lots of things in a limited amount of detail. Remember, a longer answer isn't always a better answer.

 You need to comment on context to get marks for AO3 (see **page vi**).

GCSE English Literature Poetry Anthology | Love and Relationships   5

PEEDL

Each paragraph should follow the PEEDL structure: point, evidence, explain, develop and link back to the question.

You may have been taught a different word such as PETAL, PEEL or PEED, but the idea behind it is exactly the same.

P — Point

Choose a feature (look at **page 5** for inspiration) and make a point that relates to the question.

Example

'Sonnet 29 — 'I think of thee!'' has a joyful tone.

E — Evidence

Support your point with evidence. This could be a direct quote (which could just be a single word), or an example paraphrased from the poem. Make sure to:

- use **inverted commas** (" ") if you are quoting directly from the poem.
- copy quotes accurately from the poem provided in the exam.
- keep quotes short and relevant.

Example

The speaker uses an exclamation mark in the phrase "Who art dearer, better!".

E — Explain

Explain how the evidence you have selected supports your point. Use linking words to help your answer flow.

This shows...	This reinforces...	This conveys...
This implies...	This hints...	This supports...
This emphasises...	This suggests...	This indicates...

Example

Exclamation marks are used to show strong emotion. Since the poem explores the speaker's love for her partner, the exclamation marks convey the speaker's sense of joy and excitement when she thinks about him.

D — Develop

Include additional information to develop your point further and comment on the effect that this has on the reader.

Example

Barrett Browning wrote this poem about her husband-to-be, Robert Browning. It was never intended to be published, so the joyful emotions in the poem are a genuine reflection of how she felt about him, and this creates a realistic sense of powerful love for the reader.

PEEDL continued

L Link

Link your paragraph back to the question, or link it to your next point.

Example

'Sonnet 29 — 'I think of thee!'' shows how powerful love can be, as it is presented as something that can bring people great joy and happiness.

Example

Here's an example PEEDL paragraph:

Both 'Sonnet 29 — 'I think of thee!'' and 'Singh Song!' are structured with a happy ending which reinforces the power of love.	This paragraph starts with a **point**
In 'Sonnet 29 — 'I think of thee!'', the speaker is reunited with her lover, and she reverses the opening line to "I do not think of thee"	Then gives an **example** from Sonnet 29 — 'I think of thee!'...
which suggests she has been able to overcome her obsessive thoughts.	Followed by an **explanation** of the example.
In 'Singh Song!', the poem ends with the couple sharing an intimate moment looking at the moon.	Then gives an **example** from Singh Song!...
The final line ends with a dash rather than a full stop which suggests that their love story isn't over and their love for each other will continue.	Followed by an **explanation** of the example.
Both these endings are satisfying for the reader, and conclude the poem with a positive tone. This positivity reflects the joy felt by the couples in the poems demonstrating how love can positively impact all those who experience it.	This **develops** the point and **links** back to the theme of the question: ideas about the power of love.

Conclusion

Finish your answer with a brief conclusion. This is the final paragraph where you summarise what you have covered in your answer.

Example

'Sonnet 29 — 'I think of thee!'' and 'Singh Song!' both present love as a strong emotion which can bring joy into people's lives. The poems were written almost 200 years apart, but the emotions felt by the couples are similar, showing the universality of the power of love.

TECHNICAL ACCURACY

To get top marks, you need to make sure your answer uses paragraphs and sophisticated vocabulary.

Paragraphs

Each PEEDL should have its own paragraph. You can signal a new paragraph by starting a new line, and either leaving a gap at the start of the new line or leaving an empty line above it.

Join your paragraphs with linking words to make your answer flow smoothly. For example, if you're adding extra points that agree with or extend your previous point, you could use:

- Firstly / Secondly / Thirdly / Finally...
- Furthermore...
- Another way that...
- In addition...

If your next point presents an alternative view, you could use:

- However...
- Whereas...
- Alternatively...
- On the other hand...
- In contrast...

Vocabulary

Your answer should be written in Standard English (the form of English that most people agree is correct), and you should avoid using slang or informal language.

- ⊕ The speaker in *Neutral Tones* is presented as being very bitter towards his ex-lover.
- ⊖ The speaker in *Neutral Tones* is presented as being very salty towards his ex-lover.

Use sophisticated, precise language to demonstrate your vocabulary and avoid sounding vague.

- ⊕ The verb "*Wrenched*" suggests their parting was painful.
- ⊖ The verb "*Wrenched*" suggests their parting was bad.

Use technical terms where appropriate to show your knowledge of poetic techniques.

- ⊕ Enjambment mimics how the speaker is continually climbing.
- ⊖ Some lines don't end with full stops which mimics how the speaker is continually climbing.

CHECKING YOUR ANSWER

You should spend five minutes reading over your answer and correcting any mistakes.

Correcting mistakes

There aren't any marks for SPaG for this question, but you should still make sure your answers are written in full sentences and structured in paragraphs with correct spelling, punctuation and grammar. If your answer is full of mistakes, the examiner might struggle to understand what you have written.

If you spot a mistake, here's how to correct what you've written neatly and carefully:

Remember to keep your handwriting legible. The examiner can't award you any marks if they're unable to read what you've written.

Correcting spelling

If you've spelt something incorrectly, carefully cross out the word and rewrite the correction above it.

> The poet uses ~~ceasura~~ caesura to create a pause which focuses the reader's attention.

Adding a missing word

If you've missed a word out, use this symbol ^ where the missing word should go and write the word above it.

> The ^ effect of the alliteration is to mimic how the speaker angrily spits out the words.

Missed paragraph break

If you've forgotten to start a new paragraph, just put // where you want the new paragraph to start.

> ... which encourages the reader to empathise with the speaker. // However, in *Eden Rock*, the speaker...

 Note

Learn how to spell tricky technical terms such as 'metaphor', 'simile' and 'onomatopoeia', so you can spell them confidently in the exam.

There aren't any SPaG marks for the anthology questions, but you should still check your answer.

WHEN WE TWO PARTED — LORD BYRON

The poem is addressed to the speaker's lover, giving it an intimate tone.

"*sever*" implies the end of the relationship was brutal and painful.

When we two parted
In silence and tears,
Half broken-hearted
To sever for years,
5   Pale grew thy cheek and cold,
Colder thy kiss;
Truly that hour foretold
Sorrow to this.

The dew of the morning
10 Sank chill on my brow –
It felt like the warning
Of what I feel now.
Thy vows are all broken,
And light is thy fame;
15 I hear thy name spoken,
And share in its shame.

They name thee before me,
A knell in mine ear;
A shudder comes o'er me –
20 Why wert thou so dear?
They know not I knew thee,
Who knew thee too well –
Long, long shall I rue thee,
Too deeply to tell.

25 In secret we met –
In silence I grieve,
That thy heart could forget,
Thy spirit deceive.
If I should meet thee
30 After long years,
How should I greet thee? –
With silence and tears.

"*silence*" implies the relationship was secret or that the couple had little to say to each other by the end.

"*Pale*" and "*cold*" are associated with death, which hints that the relationship was dying.

The consonance of the 'k' sound suggests that the speaker is spitting these lines out angrily, reinforcing his bitterness.

This means 'your reputation is damaged', which suggests that people have found out about the affair and his lover has been disgraced.

This could refer to the lover's vows to the speaker, or her marriage vows to her husband. Either way, it suggests that she is deceitful.

The alliteration of "*share in its shame*" repeats the 'sh' sound which reinforces the secretive nature of their relationship.

The rhetorical question suggests the speaker is confused and he struggles to move on.

"*knell*" links the end of the relationship to death, and the grief that the speaker feels when he hears his lover's name.

Although people have found out that she has been unfaithful, they do not know the identity of her lover. "*knew*" is also a euphemism meaning 'to have sex with'.

The speaker's use of hyperbole reflects his regret but also suggests he is prone to exaggeration.

The speaker feels his lover deceived him. This reinforces his bitterness towards her.

The speaker repeats line 2. This gives the poem a cyclical structure, suggesting the speaker's heartbreak is ongoing.

? **light** — unsubstantial
fame — reputation
knell — the sound of a ringing bell, especially for a funeral
rue — regret

Lord Byron

Lord Byron (1788–1824) was an English **Romantic** poet.

Lord Byron

The Romantic movement spanned the late 18th century and the first half of the 19th century. Romantic poems were often inspired by nature and prioritised emotions over logic and reason.

During his lifetime, Lord Byron was involved in several scandalous love affairs. It is thought that *When We Two Parted* (published in 1816) was an **autobiographical** poem inspired by an affair that he had in 1813 with Lady Frances Webster, a married woman. Byron pretended he had written the poem in 1808 to protect her identity.

Comment: Frances was later rumoured to have had an affair with the Duke of Wellington, which hurt Byron's pride. The gossiping in *When We Two Parted* ("*I hear thy name spoken, / And share in its shame*") could refer to the scandal resulting from Frances' supposed affair with the Duke, and the bitterness expressed by the speaker could reflect Byron's jealousy towards Frances moving on to another lover.

Summary of the poem

The speaker reflects on a love affair that has ended. He is upset because his lover broke off the relationship. There are hints that his lover was married, and that people have discovered she had been unfaithful. The scandal of the affair has damaged her reputation, however, no one knows the identity of her lover, so the speaker pretends that their relationship never happened. The speaker believes he will mourn the break-up for years to come.

Context and references

Reputation

In the 19th century, upper- and middle-class people were preoccupied with maintaining a 'good' reputation. This meant behaving in a socially acceptable way.

Married couples were expected to stay faithful, however, wives would tolerate their husbands having affairs, as long as they were discreet. It was considered unacceptable for a woman to cheat on her husband, and an affair could destroy a woman's reputation.

A wife at home while her husband secretly kisses another woman.

Comment: In the poem, it's implied that the speaker's lover is a married woman, and that her reputation is damaged when people find out about the affair ("*light is thy fame*").

Themes

Loss and heartbreak

When We Two Parted explores the negative emotions felt at the end of a relationship, including shame, bitterness, misery and jealousy.

Death

The speaker uses imagery associated with death (see **page 14**) to describe the dying relationship and to reinforce the speaker's grief as he mourns the break-up.

Romantic love

The poem focuses on a romantic relationship.

Distance

The poem explores the emotional distance between the "*parted*" couple.

Form and structure

The poem is made up of four stanzas, each with eight lines which use a regular, alternating ABAB rhyme scheme. This regular structure could suggest that the speaker feels confined by his emotions, and he cannot escape his heartbreak.

Comment: The rhyme scheme also reinforces the speaker's overwhelming sadness by rhyming significant words such as "*grieve*" and "*deceive*", "*years*" and "*tears*".

The poem is written in the first person, which creates an intimate, personal connection between the speaker and the reader.

Archaic pronouns

The speaker uses second-person pronouns that had largely fallen out of use by the time the poem was written: "*thy*" which means 'your', "*thee*" which means 'you' and "*mine*" which means 'my'. Although these pronouns weren't often used in everyday speech and writing in the 1800s, they could be found in poems, as they were considered more literary and more romantic than 'you' and 'your'.

Comment: Archaic pronouns can also be seen in *Love's Philosophy* (**page 18**) and *Sonnet 29 — 'I think of thee!'* (**page 34**).

The poem jumps between the past ("*When we two parted*"), the present ("*A shudder comes o'er me*") and the future ("*If I should meet thee*"). This suggests that the speaker's past, present and future are affected by the end of the relationship.

The poem has a **cyclic** structure: it ends in a similar way to the start by repeating the phrase "*silence and tears*". This suggests that the speaker struggles to get over the relationship. Readers may find this ending unsatisfying as there is no indication the speaker will be able to move on.

Tone

The poem is addressed to the speaker's ex-lover and explores personal emotions, which creates an intimate tone. The reader may feel as though they are reading a private poem, which was only intended for the speaker's ex-lover.

The poem has a miserable tone. The speaker is overwhelmed by negative emotions: sadness, anger and bitterness.

Language

Representation of the relationship

The speaker focuses on the unhappiness caused by the end of the relationship and doesn't reflect on happier times that the couple might have shared. This emphasises how he is consumed by heartbreak.

One-sided

The end of the relationship seems to have affected the speaker more deeply than his lover. The line "*Half-broken hearted*" implies that he was broken hearted by the end of the relationship, but his lover wasn't. This is reinforced by her kiss becoming "*Colder*", suggesting that she was losing interest in the relationship.

Comment: The speaker repeats the hard 'k' sound in the lines: "*thy chee**k** and **c**old, / **C**older thy **k**iss*". This suggests that the speaker is angrily spitting out these words, suggesting his bitterness towards his ex-lover.

Strained

The speaker uses **sensory** language to present the strained nature of their relationship.

The speaker hears "*silence*".

Comment: This suggests the couple had little to say to each other, implying that the spark between them has died.

The speaker sees his lover's "*Pale*" cheek.

His lover's cheek feels "*cold*".

Comment: Warm, pink cheeks can suggest pleasure or desire, so a cold, colourless cheek suggests that his lover no longer finds the relationship passionate or exciting, and she has lost interest in the speaker.

Language continued

Representation of the relationship continued

Secretive

The couple met in "*secret*", which implies they were having an affair. Since no one else knew about the relationship, the speaker mourns the end of the relationship in "*silence*".

Comment: The speaker's silence about the relationship contrasts with the other people gossiping about his ex-lover ("*I hear thy name spoken*").

In line 16, the phrase "*share in its shame*" repeats the 'sh' sound. This mimics the hushed sound of whispers and the secretive nature of the relationship.

Death imagery

The speaker uses imagery associated with death to reinforce that the relationship is over and the couple will not be able to reconcile. The speaker's lover is described as having a "*Pale*" and "*cold*" cheek which reminds the reader of a corpse. The speaker uses a **metaphor** to compare hearing his lover's name to a "*knell*", the sound of a funeral bell. Likening the end of the relationship to death helps to explain the speaker's grief.

Representation of the speaker

Miserable

The speaker cried when the relationship ended and felt "*Sorrow*". The speaker uses the word "*sever*" to describe their break-up, which implies it was painful and brutal.

Comment: Poems by Romantic poets, such as Byron, focused on extreme emotions, so the feelings of despair were typical of this literary movement. Romantic poets were often seen as 'tortured souls', and unhappiness could be a source of inspiration.

Bitter

The speaker's attitude changes in the third stanza, and he becomes increasingly bitter towards his ex-lover. The **rhetorical question** "*Why wert thou so dear?*" suggests he struggles to imagine how he could have ever been in love with her, and he says he will "*rue*" (regret) their relationship.

Comment: The speaker's bitterness could be caused by his jealousy. If the poem is about Lady Frances Webster's affair with the Duke of Wellington, Byron may have been hurt that she moved on to someone else.

Language continued

Representation of the speaker continued

Melodramatic

The speaker's reaction to the end of the relationship could be interpreted as melodramatic. He imagines he will greet his lover with "*silence and tears*" even after "*long years*": he doesn't think he will move on from the heartbreak even years later.

> **Comment:** His imaginary reaction to a future meeting also suggests he wants his lover to see how hurt he was by the end of the relationship, and he wants her to feel guilty.

The hyperbolic lines "*Long, long shall I rue thee, / Too deeply to tell*" present the speaker as someone prone to exaggeration because he cannot express how much he regrets the relationship. The repetition of "*long*" implies he will bear this grudge for many years.

> **Comment:** Even though the poem was written over 100 years ago, the speaker's complicated feelings towards his ex-lover are still relevant today, and many people who have experienced heartbreak will be able to sympathise with the speaker.

Representation of the speaker's lover

Deceptive

The speaker suggests that his lover is deceitful, commenting that she has "*broken*" her "*vows*". He reinforces this on line 28 with the phrase "*Thy spirit deceive*". He believes that he was deceived by her affection towards him.

> **Comment:** Since the speaker has been emotionally affected by the end of the relationship, his negative opinion of his ex-lover may be biased, and he may be an unreliable narrator.

Disgraced

It's implied that other people have found out about the affair ("*I hear thy name spoken*"), which has ruined the lover's reputation ("*light is thy fame*"). It was typical in the 19th century for unfaithful women to be treated more harshly than men (see **page 11**).

COMPARING *WHEN WE TWO PARTED*

Here's how *When We Two Parted* could be compared to other poems.

Remember, you can compare *When We Two Parted* with any poem from the anthology as long as your response is supported with examples. The following examples suggest ways to compare the poems, but they are not complete answers.

Romantic Poets

When We Two Parted was written by Lord Byron, a Romantic Poet. Romantic poetry often focused on extreme emotions, and this can be seen in *When We Two Parted*, as the speaker is overwhelmed by his feelings of despair, anger and bitterness following a break-up. His emotions could be interpreted as melodramatic. He states *"Long, long shall I rue thee"*. The repetition of *"long"* reflects the resentful tone, and the following line, *"Too deeply to tell"* is hyperbolic, reinforcing the speaker's exaggerated emotions.

Love's Philosophy (see **page 18**) was also written by a Romantic poet, Percy Bysshe Shelley, and similarly uses exaggeration to convey extreme emotions. The speaker is overwhelmed by feelings of desire and uses hyperbole to convince his lover to be physically intimate with him. The speaker compares their connection to the *"winds of heaven"*. Suggesting their relationship has religious significance shows the speaker's tendency to exaggerate, and how eager he is to persuade his lover to kiss him.

Secretive relationships

When We Two Parted is thought to be about Lord Byron's relationship with Lady Frances Webster, a married woman. After their affair ended, Webster supposedly had an affair with the Duke of Wellington, which eventually became public knowledge. This is reflected in the lines, *"And light is thy fame; / I hear thy name spoken"*. The poem's autobiographical nature makes the speaker's grief and bitterness seem more genuine and intense. Byron lied about when he wrote the poem to protect Lady Webster's identity and therefore her reputation.

Sonnet 29 — 'I think of thee!' (see **page 34**) is also believed to be about a secretive relationship between Elizabeth Barrett Browning, and her future husband, Robert. Elizabeth's father forbade her from marrying, so she kept their relationship hidden until after they were married. However, rather than focusing on the end of a relationship *Sonnet 29 — 'I think of thee!'* examines the longing that some people feel at the start of a relationship by using an extended metaphor to compare the speaker's obsessive thoughts to vines that wrap around a tree. Similarly to *When We Two Parted*, Barrett Browning also attempted to disguise her personal connection to the poem. She initially claimed that she had translated it from another language to protect the identities of her and Robert.

Compare how poets present ideas about the end of romantic relationships in *When We Two Parted* and in **one** other poem from Love and Relationships. [30 marks]

Your answer may include:

AO1 — show understanding of the poems

- 'When We Two Parted' and 'Neutral Tones' focus on the emotions felt following the end of a romantic relationship. In both poems, the speaker's lover has lost interest in them, resulting in heartbreak. Both poems suggest that the end of a romantic relationship can negatively affect someone for many years.

AO2 — show understanding of the poets' language choices

- Both speakers use language associated with death to describe the end of the relationship. In 'When We Two Parted', the speaker says, "Pale grew thy cheek and cold". The image of a cold, pale cheek has connotations of a corpse, emphasising how the love, and life, has disappeared from their relationship. Similarly, in 'Neutral Tones', the speaker comments that his lover's smile is the "deadest thing" to reinforce how the affection between them has died. Using imagery associated with death helps the reader to understand how heartbreak can feel like grief.

- Both poems use a cyclical structure. In 'When We Two Parted', the speaker repeats the phrase "silence and tears" from line 2 in the final line of the poem. Similarly, in 'Neutral Tones', the speaker recalls the "pond" from the first line in the final line of the poem. In both poems, this repetition reinforces how the heartbreak continues to affect them and how they struggle to move on. This creates an unsatisfying conclusion for the reader as both poems end with a pessimistic tone.

- In both poems, the speaker addresses their former lover directly. This creates an intimate tone, and makes the reader feel as though they are prying into something personal. Addressing the ex-lovers directly also suggests that both speakers wanted their former partners to understand how hurt they were by the break-up and to make them feel guilty.

AO3 — relate the poems to the context

- 'When We Two' Parted is believed to be about Byron's affair with Lady Frances Webster, and Thomas Hardy was unlucky in love throughout his life. The autobiographical nature of the poems adds to their realism, as both speakers convey cynical and pessimistic attitudes towards love following the end of their romantic relationships.

This answer should be marked in accordance with the levels-based mark scheme on page 134.

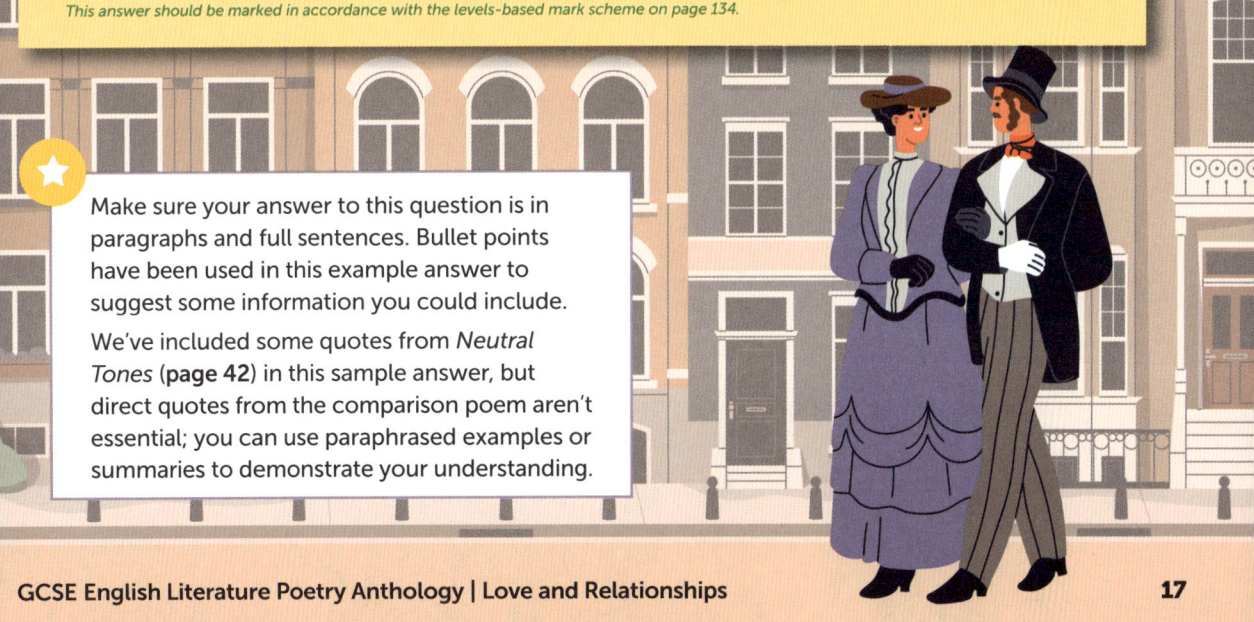

⭐ Make sure your answer to this question is in paragraphs and full sentences. Bullet points have been used in this example answer to suggest some information you could include.

We've included some quotes from *Neutral Tones* (**page 42**) in this sample answer, but direct quotes from the comparison poem aren't essential; you can use paraphrased examples or summaries to demonstrate your understanding.

LOVE'S PHILOSOPHY — PERCY BYSSHE SHELLEY

The speaker explains that water from a fountain (spring) flows into rivers and oceans. He implies that something small can be part of something bigger.

The speaker uses natural imagery throughout the poem to persuade his lover that an intimate relationship is also natural.

The speaker presents opinions as facts to make his argument seem more persuasive.

The speaker's argument builds to a rhetorical question, suggesting that he expects the reader to be persuaded by his argument.

The speaker goes even further to suggest that God could not forgive a couple who weren't intimate.

The fountains mingle with the river
And the rivers with the ocean,
The winds of heaven mix for ever
With a sweet emotion;
5   Nothing in the world is single;
All things by a law divine
In one another's being mingle —
Why not I with thine?

See the mountains kiss high heaven,
10 And the waves clasp one another;
No sister-flower would be forgiven
If it disdain'd its brother:
And the sunlight clasps the earth,
And the moonbeams kiss the sea —
15 What are all these kisses worth,
If thou kiss not me?

Comparing their connection to the "*winds of heaven*" gives religious significance to an intimate relationship.

Referring to a "*law divine*" suggests that their union would be blessed by God.

The speaker uses a dash to create a pause before the rhetorical question. This helps the question stand out from the rest of the stanza.

The speaker uses personification to suggest that physical touch is natural.

The speaker repeats the words "*clasp*" and "*kiss*" to reinforce his desire.

? **philosophy** — the study of reality and existence
fountain — source of a spring   **disdain'd** — spurned

Percy Bysshe Shelley

Percy Bysshe Shelley (1792–1822) was an English **Romantic** poet (see **page 11**). Shelley believed in 'free love', which was very controversial at the time. He didn't believe in monogamy (the idea of being in a relationship with one person at time) and thought that both men and women should be allowed to have sex before marriage. He wrote *Love's Philosophy* in 1819.

> **Comment:** The poem could present Shelley's philosophy about free love, and sexual relationships outside marriage.

Percy Bysshe Shelley

Summary of the poem

The speaker tries to convince his lover to have a physical relationship with him by giving examples of interconnectedness found in nature. The speaker claims that God intended for everything in nature to "*mingle*", so God would approve of their physical relationship.

Context and references

Courtship: Finding a wife or husband in the early 19th century (especially for the upper classes) was very different to today. Couples could get engaged within days of meeting each other, and there were certain rules that they had to follow.

- Unmarried men and women could only meet in the presence of a chaperone (someone who would supervise the meeting, usually a married woman) to avoid any rumours that the couple had behaved improperly.
- Any 'improper' behaviour (which included kissing and hand-holding) could ruin a woman's reputation, and the man responsible would be expected to marry the woman to 'save' her reputation.

Ladies and a suitor at a ball, with two chaperones sat on the sofa.

> **Comment:** The speaker's lover may be reluctant to kiss him because it may ruin her reputation.

Religion: Most people in early-nineteenth-century Britain were Christians who followed the teachings of the Bible. Christian beliefs influenced romantic relationships: men and women were taught that sex was only acceptable between married couples.

> **Comment:** The speaker tries to persuade his lover to be intimate with him by claiming God would approve. This makes the speaker's intentions seem purer, and may have been more convincing to a 19th-century reader.

Themes

Romantic love

The poem focuses on romantic love between the speaker and his lover. The speaker tries to convince his lover to kiss him with a playful argument.

Nature

The speaker uses examples from nature, such as the ocean, mountains and sunlight, to convince his lover that an intimate relationship is natural.

Religion

The speaker claims God made everything in nature, and these things interconnect, therefore God would approve of their intimate relationship.

Form and structure

The poem is made up of two eight-line stanzas which use an alternating ABAB rhyme scheme. The speaker may have used a pair of stanzas and pairs of rhyming lines to reinforce the idea of couples in unity. The regular rhyme scheme suggests that the speaker's love is unwavering, and he is committed to his lover.

Comment: The first and third lines of both stanzas use half rhymes ("*river*" and "*ever*", "*heaven*" and "*forgiven*"). This could reflect how the speaker and his lover aren't yet physically united.

The speaker uses **enjambment** throughout the poem, for example, across lines 1 and 2. This structural device reinforces the poem's concept of unity: the lines in the poem are connected, just like the examples found in nature.

The poem is written in the first person, and is addressed to the speaker's lover. This creates an intimate tone, as the reader may feel that they are reading something private.

Each stanza is structured to be as persuasive as possible to encourage the speaker's lover to kiss him. The speaker gives examples of connections found in nature and explains that these connections are approved by God. Since 19th-century society was Christian (see **page 19**), using religion in this way may have made the poem seem more convincing. Both stanzas end with a **rhetorical question**, which encourages the lover to reply to the speaker.

Comment: Philosophy is the study of reality, existence and human nature, and it can also refer to an individual's system of beliefs. The title suggests that the speaker is presenting his own beliefs about love, and calling them a 'philosophy' makes them seem more convincing.

Tone

The poem has a persuasive tone. The speaker is trying to convince his lover to kiss him by suggesting they have a duty to be together because there are so many examples of unity in the natural world.

Love's Philosophy could also be interpreted as having a playful tone. The speaker may suspect he is unlikely to convince his lover to kiss him, but he cheekily tries to persuade her anyway.

Comment: The tone could also be interpreted as manipulative. The speaker is prepared to exploit his lover's religious beliefs to get his own way.

Language

Persuasive language techniques

The speaker uses techniques that are more commonly found in persuasive writing.

Declaratives

Many of the poem's lines are written as **declaratives**: sentences used to present information. The speaker uses this sentence form to state opinions as facts. For example, *"Nothing in the world is single"* is an opinion, but the speaker presents it as a fact. This makes the speaker's argument seem more forceful and persuasive.

Rhetorical questions

Both stanzas build to a **rhetorical question** which invites the reader to agree with the speaker. The speaker includes a pause before each rhetorical question (indicated by a dash) to make the question stand out from the rest of the poem.

Comment: Both rhetorical questions are made up of five syllables. These lines are shorter than the other lines of the poem which gives them more emphasis.

Language continued

Natural language

Comment: Romantic poets like Shelley were influenced by nature. Shelley may have used natural imagery to reinforce his belief that 'free love' was also natural.

The speaker uses lots of examples of natural imagery in the poem, including rivers, oceans, the wind, mountains, flowers and sunlight. These examples suggest an intimate relationship would also be natural and beautiful.

Comment: The examples of interconnectedness could be interpreted as **euphemisms** (politer terms) for sex. Talking openly about sex was taboo in the early 1800s, so the speaker may have used natural imagery to disguise his desire.

The first line repeats the short 'i' sound: "*The fountains mingle with the river*". This **assonance** creates a pleasing rhythm, and introduces the idea that all things are interconnected.

The speaker also **personifies** nature (e.g. "*the mountains kiss high heaven*"). This suggests that connections in nature are deliberate and purposeful, not accidental or random.

The speaker uses **anaphora**, repeating the phrase "*And the*" on lines 2, 10, 13 and 14. This makes the list of examples found in nature seem longer and his argument more persuasive.

Religious language

Comment: Shelley was expelled from Oxford University for writing an essay on atheism (the belief that there is no God), so it's ironic he uses God to try to convince his lover to kiss him. This suggests that he's prepared to say anything to persuade her.

The speaker uses religious language such as "*heaven*" and "*law divine*" to persuade his lover that God approves of physical affection. This makes the speaker's feelings seem pure, rather than lustful.

Comment: The speaker compares a physical relationship to something heavenly. This is an example of **hyperbole**: the speaker exaggerates the significance of their relationship to make his argument seem more persuasive.

The speaker takes his religious argument one step further in the second stanza when he says: "*No sister-flower would be forgiven / If it disdain'd its brother*". This line implies that God couldn't forgive a woman who wouldn't embrace her brother. Introducing the idea of 'unforgivable' behaviour may convince the speaker's lover to kiss him rather than disobey God.

Comment: Introducing a brother-sister relationship presents the speaker's intentions as innocent and affectionate, rather than sexual, and makes the speaker's argument seem less forceful and intense.

Language continued

Language of connections

The speaker includes language from the semantic field of togetherness to reinforce the message that the couple should be physically intimate. This language is initially gentle ("*mingle*", "*mix*" and "*meet*"), but becomes more intense and sexual in the second stanza, with "*kiss*" and "*clasp*". This reflects the speaker's increasing desire towards his lover.

> **Comment:** The word "*kiss*" is repeated in the final three lines of the poem, reinforcing the speaker's intentions.

Representation of the speaker

It's unclear whether the speaker genuinely believes the argument he is presenting, or if he thinks using examples from religion and nature is the most likely way to convince his lover to give into him. Focusing his argument on nature and religion makes his desire seem pure and genuine, rather than sexual.

Although it's assumed that the speaker is a man addressing a woman (reinforced by the genders used in "*sister-flower*" and "*brother*") there is no direct evidence of the gender of either the speaker or their lover. Although Shelley married a woman, his belief in 'free love' and his close relationships with other men have been interpreted by some as evidence of his bisexuality.

COMPARING *LOVE'S PHILOSOPHY*

Here's how *Love's Philosophy* could be compared to other poems.

Remember, you can compare *Love's Philosophy* with any poem from the anthology as long as your response is supported with examples. The following examples suggest ways to compare the poems, but they are not complete answers.

Attitudes towards sexual love

Love's Philosophy focuses on the importance of desire and physical intimacy in a romantic relationship. However, the poem was written in the 1800s, when sex was considered a taboo subject, particularly amongst the upper classes. As a result, the speaker uses natural imagery as euphemisms for sex to disguise his intentions, such as the "*fountains mingle with the river*" and the "*winds of heaven mix forever*". Shelley also believed in 'free love' and sex outside of marriage. He may have chosen imagery from nature to present physical intimacy as something pure and natural rather than something sinful and distasteful.

Singh Song! (see **pages 114–115**) also explores desire in a romantic relationship. However, this poem was written 200 years after *Love's Philosophy*, so the speaker's attitudes towards sexual intimacy are more progressive and liberal. The speaker bluntly states "*vee have made luv / like vee rowing through Putney*". This simile presents the couple's lovemaking as vigorous, but the comical comparison also suggests that it is joyful. The speaker doesn't use euphemistic language, suggesting that he is not ashamed of his desire, which reflects society's more liberal attitude towards sex.

Natural imagery

Love's Philosophy uses vibrant natural imagery to represent an intimate relationship. For example, the speaker uses personification to describe how the "*mountains kiss high heaven*". This makes the mountains come alive by implying that their actions are deliberate and purposeful, and the verb "*kiss*" reinforces the intimate tone. Personification is also used in the line "*waves clasp one another*". The dynamic movement of the waves embracing presents love as something exhilarating, which reinforces the lively and romantic tone of the poem.

Neutral Tones (see **page 42**) also uses natural imagery, but rather than presenting love as something intimate and dynamic, the speaker uses it to present love as something painful and depressing. The speaker uses personification in the phrase "*starving sod*" which suggests the ground is suffering. This image reflects the couple's dying relationship, and reinforces the pessimistic tone of the poem.

Compare how poets present ideas about romantic love in *Love's Philosophy* and in **one** other poem from Love and Relationships.

[30 marks]

Your answer may include:

AO1 — show understanding of the poems

- In both 'Love's Philosophy' and 'The Farmer's Bride', the speakers crave intimacy with their romantic partners. In 'Love's Philosophy', the speaker tries to persuade his lover to "kiss" him. However, in 'The Farmer's Bride', the speaker describes how his bride refuses to speak to him or show him any affection. Although both poems are about longing and desire, they have very different attitudes towards romantic love. In 'Love's Philosophy', love is presented as playful and light-hearted, whereas love is presented as frustrating and hurtful in 'The Farmer's Bride'.

AO2 — show understanding of the poets' language choices

- In 'Love's Philosophy', the poem is addressed to the speaker's lover, using the second-person pronoun "thou". Archaic pronouns were sometimes used in the 19th century to add to the romantic and poetic mood of a text. This personal address creates a sense of intimacy between the speaker and the addressee, suggesting their romantic relationship is private and confidential. On the other hand, 'The Farmer's Bride' is a dramatic monologue written in the first person. The farmer addresses his wife using the third-person pronoun "she" which reinforces how the farmer struggles to communicate with his wife directly, and emphasises the distance and conflict in their relationship.

- In 'Love's Philosophy', the speaker creates a playful tone by constructing an oversimplified argument to convince his love to "kiss" him. The speaker argues that they should be physically intimate because everything in nature is connected. The speaker uses increasingly suggestive verbs. He begins with "mingle" and "mix" in the first stanza, which progresses to the more sexual "clasp" and "kiss" in the second stanza, reinforcing his desire. However, in 'The Farmer's Bride', the speaker creates a miserable tone. The farmer is unhappy because he's "hardly heard her speak", and the alliteration of the 'h' in this phrase mimics a sighing sound, which emphasises the farmer's sense of despair.

AO3 — relate the poems to the context

- Both poems suggest that sexual intimacy is an important aspect of romantic relationships, however, the speakers' attitudes towards sex reflect attitudes of the day. In the early 1800s when 'Love's Philosophy' was written, it was improper to talk about sex, and it was taboo for women to have sex outside of marriage so the speaker uses euphemisms such as "the sunlight clasps the earth" to disguise his desire for sexual intimacy. In 'The Farmer's Bride', it's implied that the bride became fearful on her wedding night. This reflects how women in the early-twentieth century were expected to be virgins when they married and were not taught about sex.

This answer should be marked in accordance with the levels-based mark scheme on page 134.

⭐ Make sure your answer to this question is in paragraphs and full sentences. Bullet points have been used in this example answer to suggest some information you could include.

We've included some quotes from *The Farmer's Bride* (**page 50**) in this sample answer, but direct quotes from the comparison poem aren't essential; you can use paraphrased examples or summaries to demonstrate your understanding.

GCSE English Literature **Poetry Anthology | LOVE AND RELATIONSHIPS**

PORPHYRIA'S LOVER — ROBERT BROWNING

The rain set early in to-night,
    The sullen wind was soon awake,
It tore the elm-tops down for spite,
    And did its worst to vex the lake:
5   I listened with heart fit to break.
When glided in Porphyria; straight
    She shut the cold out and the storm,
And kneeled and made the cheerless grate
    Blaze up, and all the cottage warm;
10 Which done, she rose, and from her form
Withdrew the dripping cloak and shawl,
    And laid her soiled gloves by, untied
Her hat and let the damp hair fall,
    And, last, she sat down by my side
15 And called me. When no voice replied,
She put my arm about her waist,
    And made her smooth white shoulder bare,
And all her yellow hair displaced,
    And, stooping, made my cheek lie there,
20 And spread o'er all her yellow hair,
Murmuring how she loved me — she
    Too weak, for all her heart's endeavour,
To set its struggling passion free
    From pride, and vainer ties dissever,
25 And give herself to me for ever.
But passion sometimes would prevail,
    Nor could to-night's gay feast restrain
A sudden thought of one so pale
    For love of her, and all in vain:
30 So, she was come through wind and rain.

Annotations:

- The speaker uses pathetic fallacy to describe the violence of the wind. This establishes an uneasy mood and foreshadows the speaker's unnecessary violence later in the poem.
- "glided" suggests Porphyria moves in an elegant, almost mysterious, way.
- Porphyria is associated with warmth, goodness and domesticity: she "shut the cold out" and starts a fire to warm the cottage. This presents her as a sympathetic character.
- Repetition of "And" at the start of the line reinforces Porphyria's activity compared to the speaker's passivity. She moves around the cottage with purpose while the speaker stays still and quiet.
- The speaker mentions her "hair" several times, showing his preoccupation with it. This foreshadows Porphyria's death later in the poem.
- Porphyria positions her lover. This foreshadows the speaker arranging Porphyria's corpse after he kills her.
- The speaker criticises Porphyria for being "weak". The speaker hints that Porphyria cannot commit to their relationship publicly because she is from a higher social class, and it wouldn't be socially acceptable for them to be together.
- This foreshadows Porphyria's murder.
- Porphyria had been at a "feast", but she left to be with her lover. This suggests that Porphyria is keen to be with the speaker.

vex — irritate **dissever** — cut
oped — opened

> Her love and devotion seem to trigger the speaker's desire to kill her.

Be sure I looked up at her eyes
    Happy and proud; at last I knew
Porphyria worshipped me; surprise
    Made my heart swell, and still it grew
35 While I debated what to do.
That moment she was **mine, mine**, fair,
    Perfectly pure and good: I found
A thing to do, and all her hair
    In one long yellow string I wound
40 **Three times her little throat** around,
And strangled her. No pain felt she;
    I am quite sure she felt no pain.
As a shut bud that holds a bee,
    I warily oped her lids: again
45 Laughed the blue eyes without a stain.
And I untightened next the tress
    About her neck; her cheek once more
Blushed bright beneath my **burning kiss**:
    I propped her head up as before,
50 Only, this time my shoulder bore
Her head, which droops upon it still:
    The smiling rosy little head,
So glad it has its utmost will,
    That all it scorned at once is fled,
55 And I, **its** love, am gained instead!
Porphyria's love: she guessed not how
    Her darling one wish would be heard.
And thus we sit together now,
    And all night long we have not stirred,
60 And yet **God has not said a word!**

> Repetition of "*mine*" reinforces the speaker's possessive nature.

> The alliterative phrase is placed at the start of the line to emphasise Porphyria's goodness. "*pure*" could be a euphemism for Porphyria being a virgin.

> Porphyria is strangled with her own hair. Since long hair is more often associated with women, the speaker uses Porphyria's femininity against her.

> This blunt statement is shocking, and the unemotional language suggests the speaker is unremorseful.

> Porphyria's face has reddened following her strangulation, but the speaker interprets her pink face as blushing. This shows he is delusional: he's misinterpreting reality to suit his own perception.

> The speaker describes his kiss as "*burning*": suggesting he associates affection with violence.

> The speaker refers to Porphyria as 'it'. The speaker dehumanises her.

> The speaker uses an exclamation mark here (and on line 60) suggesting that the murder has excited him.

> The ending is shocking: not only did the speaker murder Porphyria, but he also sat with her posed corpse all evening. There is no suggestion that the speaker will be punished for what he has done.

> The speaker remarks that God has not punished him for his actions. He interprets this as having God's blessing, or hinting that there is no God.

GCSE English Literature Poetry Anthology | Love and Relationships

Robert Browning

Robert Browning (1812–1889) was an English poet and playwright. He published *Porphyria's Lover* in 1836.

Robert Browning married the poet Elizabeth Barrett Browning, see **page 34**.

In the 19th century, women were often seen as the 'property' of their husbands, and domestic violence was not only commonplace, but also socially acceptable. Browning was politically liberal, and he supported more rights for women.

Robert Browning

Comment: Browning may have used *Porphyria's Lover* to explore what was considered more shocking to readers: a woman showing sexual desire or a man killing his lover.

Summary of the poem

On a wet and windy evening, the speaker waits in a cottage for his lover, Porphyria, to arrive. Porphyria enters, and lights a fire. She removes her wet clothing and approaches the speaker, putting his head on her shoulder. She tells the speaker that she loves him. The speaker strangles Porphyria with her own hair. After killing her, he poses her corpse and sits with it all night. The speaker remarks that God has not punished him for murdering Porphyria.

Context and references

Porphyria

Porphyria is the name given to a group of liver disorders. Symptoms include anxiety, hallucinations, mental confusion and sensitivity to sunlight.

Comment: One interpretation of the poem is that the speaker is suffering from porphyria, and he hallucinates the encounter, or he suffers a bout of madness which causes him to murder his lover.

Social status

In the 19th century, British society was divided into three classes: lower, middle and upper class. Men and women were expected to marry someone from their own class. Being romantically involved with someone from a lower social class could cause a scandal.

Comment: The speaker comments on Porphyria's "*pride, and vainer ties*", which suggests she is from a higher social class than the speaker. This could explain why they can't be seen together in public.

Women in the early 19th century

Women in the 1800s were careful to protect their reputations (see **page 11**). It is likely that Porphyria and her lover meet in secret because they are unmarried, or they are having an affair. If their relationship was discovered, it would have ruined Porphyria's reputation.

Themes

Obsession and control
The speaker murders Porphyria because he wants to own and control her.

Romantic love
The couple conduct their romantic relationship in secret.

Religion
The speaker believes God approves of the murder because God hasn't *"said a word"*. The speaker uses religion to justify his actions.

Death
Porphyria is murdered by her lover.

Form and structure

The poem is a **dramatic monologue**: it is written in the first person, and told from the perspective of the speaker, Porphyria's lover. There isn't any direct speech, and the events of the poem unfold in one uninterrupted stanza, reinforcing the poem as the speaker's stream of conscious.

The poem has an ABABB rhyme scheme, and this unbalanced rhyme scheme reinforces the speaker's mental instability.

The poem uses **foreshadowing** (hinting at things that will happen later in the poem) to create an unsettling tone and suggest that Porphyria's murder was unavoidable. For example:

During the stormy weather, the wind is described as damaging trees out of *"spite"*.		This foreshadows how the speaker kills Porphyria for no reason.
Porphyria arranges her lover, positioning his hand on her waist and moving his cheek on to her shoulder.		This foreshadows how the speaker positions Porphyria's body after her murder.
The speaker is fixated by Porphyria's hair, mentioning it three times (on line 13, 18 and 20).		This foreshadows the speaker strangling Porphyria with her own hair.
The speaker believes that Porphyria is committed to him, and wants to give herself to him *"for ever"*.		The speaker murders Porphyria so that he 'owns' her forever.

The poem's ending is unsatisfying. The speaker shows no remorse and God doesn't say *"a word"*, which suggests the speaker won't be punished for the murder.

Tone

The poem has an unsettling and uncomfortable tone. The uneasy tone is introduced with the **personification** of the unpleasant, stormy weather. The disturbing tone reaches a climax when Porphyria is strangled, and the speaker poses her corpse and sits with it all night.

Comment: The description of the "*sullen wind*" is an example of **pathetic fallacy**, where something not human is given human emotions.

Language

Representation of the speaker

Passive

Although the speaker narrates the story, he does very little until he strangles Porphyria. At the start of the poem, he sits alone in the cottage, just listening. When Porphyria enters and speaks to him, he ignores her ("*When no voice replied*"). Porphyria arranges the speaker by putting his arm around her waist and putting his cheek on her shoulder. This presents the speaker as passive and disinterested in Porphyria. However, his inactivity may remind readers of predators who lie in wait for their prey, drawing them closer before they pounce.

Comment: In the early 1800s, men were seen as the dominant sex, and women were thought of as 'weaker' and 'lesser' than men. At first, Porphyria seems to control the speaker, which subverts typical gender stereotypes of the time.

Psychopathic

The speaker murders Porphyria to keep her "*Perfectly pure*", which suggests he kills her so she stays a virgin forever. Using alliteration and placing this phrase at the start of the line emphasises its importance to the speaker.

> Women in the 19th century (especially those from the upper classes) were expected to be virgins when they married. Virginity was associated with moral and religious purity.

Despite committing murder, he calmly sits with her body "*all night long*" suggesting that he doesn't feel remorse. He only shows affection towards Porphyria when she's dead, for example, by kissing her cheek. This distressing behaviour is unnatural and suggests the speaker is mentally unwell.

Comment: The speaker comments how Porphyria "*Blushed*" when he kissed her, perceiving her flushed face as a sign of delight. However, Porphyria's face is red because she was strangled. This suggests the speaker is delusional and has lost grip on reality.

Language continued

Representation of Porphyria

Comment: Although the poem focuses on Porphyria, the reader never hears her speak. Porphyria's voicelessness reinforces her powerlessness, and represents how the speaker controls her.

Devoted

Since unmarried men and women couldn't spend time together alone in the 1800s, Porphyria risks her reputation to be with him, emphasising her devotion.

Warm-hearted

When Porphyria enters the room, she makes a fire "*Blaze*" in the "*cheerless grate*", which symbolises her warm, caring nature. She is affectionate towards the speaker and tells him that she loves him. Presenting Porphyria as warm and loving makes her murder seem even more shocking, as it is completely unprovoked.

Sexual

Porphyria is presented as having sexual desire. She removes her clothes in front of her lover, bares her "*smooth white shoulder*" and encourages him to touch her waist.

Comment: Women in the 1800s weren't expected to show sexual desire, so Porphyria's sexuality would have been shocking at the time. Some Victorian readers may have believed that Porphyria 'got what she deserved' for her 'immoral' behaviour.

Representation of the speaker's attitude towards Porphyria

Possessive language

The speaker uses possessive language to describe Porphyria. He refers to her as "*mine, mine*", where the repetition of the possessive pronoun reinforces ownership. The speaker wants to possess Porphyria "*for ever*", showing the extent of his obsession.

Diminutive language

The speaker comments that Porphyria has a "*little throat*" and a "*little head*". This implies that killing Porphyria has made the speaker feel large and powerful: he's no longer threatened by Porphyria and her sexuality.

Flower imagery

The speaker compares Porphyria's body to a wilting flower. She is a "*shut bud*", her skin is "*rosy*" and her head "*droops*". Flowers are usually associated with life, so it's unsettling that the speaker uses floral imagery to describe her corpse.

Comment: The flower imagery represents the speaker's feelings towards Porphyria: she is beautiful, but fragile. Like a plucked flower, she will begin to decompose.

COMPARING *PORPHYRIA'S LOVER*

Here's how *Porphyria's Lover* could be compared to other poems.

Remember, you can compare *Porphyria's Lover* with any poem from the anthology as long as your response is supported with examples. The following examples suggest ways to compare the poems, but they are not complete answers.

Representations of death

In *Porphyria's Lover*, the speaker murders his lover, Porphyria. Following her death, he uses language to imply that she is still alive. For example, the speaker says her eyes "*Laughed*", suggesting that she is happy. He also describes how her cheeks "*Blushed*" when he kisses her, suggesting that she still feels desire and pleasure for the speaker. Using language associated with life when Porphyria is deceased presents the speaker as disturbed.

On the other hand, the speaker in *When We Two Parted* (see **page 10**) uses language associated with death to describe the living. The speaker comments "*Pale grew thy cheek and cold*", which compares his lover to a corpse with a bloodless and cold cheek. The imagery associated with death continues when the speaker says that hearing his lover's name is like a "*knell*": the sound of a funeral bell. Using language associated with death to describe his lover reinforces the speaker's grief following the end of the relationship.

Natural Imagery

In *Porphyria's Lover*, the speaker uses natural imagery to describe Porphyria after he murders her. He compares her to a "*shut bud*" and describes her "*rosy little head*" that "*droops*". The speaker's choice of language suggests that he views her as beautiful, but also small and fragile, like a wilting flower. This reinforces how he enjoys feeling more powerful than Porphyria, and he seems delighted that he can finally control her.

The speaker in *Walking Away* (see **page 58**) uses natural imagery to describe the fragility of his son. The speaker compares his son to a "*half-fledged thing*", suggesting that he is like a delicate baby bird that isn't quite strong enough to fly the nest. Similar to *Porphyria's Lover*, the speaker's choice of language suggests that he feels more powerful than his son. However, unlike in *Porphyria's Lover*, the speaker in *Walking Away* wants to protect his son, rather than control him.

Compare how poets present ideas about obsessive love in *Porphyria's Lover* and in **one** other poem from Love and Relationships. [30 marks]

Your answer may include:

AO1 — show understanding of the poems

- Both 'Porphyria's Lover' and 'Sonnet 29 — 'I think of thee!'' are told from the perspective of speakers who are experiencing obsessive love. However, the way the speakers deal with their obsession, and the resolution of the poems, are very different. In 'Porphyria's Lover', the speaker's obsession drives him to 'own' Porphyria by murdering her. The speaker in 'Sonnet 29 — 'I think of thee!'' is overwhelmed by thoughts of her lover, however, she regains control of her obsessive love by being in the presence of her partner.

AO2 — show understanding of the poets' language choices

- Both speakers use natural imagery, however, the tone created by the imagery is different. In 'Porphyria's Lover', the speaker uses pathetic fallacy to describe the "sullen wind" that "tore the elm-tops down for spite". Presenting nature as destructive creates an unsettling tone and hints that something bad may happen. However, in 'Sonnet 29 — 'I think of thee!'', the speaker uses an extended metaphor of vines wrapping around a palm tree to explain how overwhelming her thoughts are. However, the imagery of growing vines presents nature as something thriving, which suggests her feelings are natural and their love is flourishing. This creates a loving, affectionate tone.

- Both poems suggest that obsessive love can be dangerous and damaging. In 'Porphyria's Lover', the speaker's obsession causes him to lose grip on reality and murder his lover. The speaker's disturbing behaviour continues as he sits with Porphyria's body all evening without showing any remorse. The speaker in 'Sonnet 29 — 'I think of thee!'' recognises that her obsession is damaging. She admits that her thoughts obscure her lover so "there's nought to see", which suggests that she has idealised him, and obscured his true nature. However, the speaker regains control and acknowledges "I will not have my thoughts instead of thee".

AO3 — relate the poems to the context

- Both poems combine obsession with sexual desire. Female sexuality was a taboo subject in the Victorian era, so women showing desire would have been shocking. In 'Porphyria's Lover', readers may have been more stunned by Porphyria making "her smooth white shoulder bare" than the violence of the speaker. Victorian readers may have thought that Porphyria deserved death for behaving in an 'immoral' way.

- The speaker in 'Sonnet 29 — 'I think of thee!'' uses a metaphor to disguise her sexual feelings. The phrase "set thy trunk all bare" could be a reference to her lover being bare chested. The speaker may have used a metaphor to avoid offending and shocking her readers.

This answer should be marked in accordance with the levels-based mark scheme on page 134.

Make sure your answer to this question is in paragraphs and full sentences. Bullet points have been used in this example answer to suggest some information you could include.

We've included some quotes from *Sonnet 29 — 'I think of thee!'* (**page 34**) in this sample answer, but direct quotes from the comparison poem aren't essential; you can use paraphrased examples or summaries to demonstrate your understanding.

SONNET 29 — 'I THINK OF THEE!' — ELIZABETH BARRETT BROWNING

The exclamation mark shows the strength of the speaker's feelings.

The word "*twine*" has sexual connotations, suggesting that the speaker is wrapped around her lover.

The speaker uses an extended metaphor, where her lover is a "*tree*" and her thoughts are "*vines*" that surround it. Using imagery from nature presents their love as something natural.

The speaker directly addresses her lover. This establishes a personal, confidential tone.

This signals the turning point (volta) of the poem.

The speaker scolds herself for obsessing over her lover. She wants to be with her lover rather than just thinking about him.

The dynamic list of three shows how she has broken free from her obsessive thoughts.

The speaker inverts the first line of the poem. This suggests that she has overcome her obsession.

I think of thee! — my thoughts do twine and bud
About thee, as wild vines, about a tree,
Put out broad leaves, and soon there's nought to see
Except the straggling green which hides the wood.
5 Yet, O my palm-tree, be it understood
I will not have my thoughts instead of thee
Who art dearer, better! Rather, instantly
Renew thy presence; as a strong tree should,
Rustle thy boughs and set thy trunk all bare,
10 And let these bands of greenery which insphere thee
Drop heavily down — burst, shattered, everywhere!
Because, in this deep joy to see and hear thee
And breathe within thy shadow a new air,
I do not think of thee — I am too near thee.

The vines cover the tree, suggesting that the speaker's thoughts about her lover are overwhelming. It could also suggest that her idealised thoughts about him have obscured his true nature.

The sibilance of the repeated 's' sound mimics the rustling of leaves.

The speaker ends lines 10, 12 and 14 with the word "*thee*" (you). This reinforces how the speaker is overwhelmed with thoughts of her lover.

The speaker acknowledges that once she is with him, she can stop obsessing over him because she is so happy to be with him.

? **twine** — entwine, wrap **nought** — nothing
insphere — enclose

Elizabeth Barrett Browning

Elizabeth Barrett Browning

Elizabeth Barrett Browning (1806–1861) was an English Romantic poet (see **page 11**). She was born to a wealthy family and wrote poetry from a young age. She suffered from ill health for most of her adult life. She met Robert Browning (see **page 28**) in 1845 and married soon after. *Sonnet 29 — 'I think of thee!'* is thought to have been written during the couple's courtship, and was an **autobiographical** poem intended for her eyes only. The poem was later published as part of a collection, *Sonnets from the Portuguese*, in 1850. The poems in the collection were numbered, hence the title Sonnet 29

Comment: Barrett Browning chose the collection's title, *Sonnets from the Portuguese*, because she wanted readers to think that the poems had been translated from another language. The poems were so personal, she didn't want readers to know she had written them.

Summary of the poem

The speaker compares her thoughts about her lover to vines that wrap around a tree. Her thoughts are so overwhelming that the vines completely obscure the tree. The speaker recognises that her thoughts are no substitute for being together, and she commands the tree to "*Rustle*" its branches, so that the vines fall away. Once the speaker is in the presence of her lover, her obsessive thoughts no longer overwhelm her.

Context and references

Elizabeth and Robert

Elizabeth and Robert

Barrett Browning's father forbade any of his children from marrying, so Elizabeth kept her relationship with Robert a secret. When her father discovered she had married, Elizabeth was disowned. Elizabeth and Robert were well-known authors, so their secret relationship and the scandal surrounding their elopement and disinheritance was widely discussed in Victorian society. The publication of *Sonnets from the Portuguese* offered readers a glimpse into Elizabeth's private feelings towards her husband.

Victorian communication

Because Elizabeth and Robert's relationship was initially a secret, the couple had limited opportunities to be together. Their relationship was made even more difficult by Elizabeth's ill health as she was often bedridden. Victorians didn't have phones, so they relied on letters to stay in touch. This meant that Elizabeth could go for days without hearing from Robert, so it's unsurprising that she could be overwhelmed by thoughts of him when they were apart.

Themes

Romantic love

The speaker is infatuated with her lover, and longs to be with him.

Distance

The speaker is physically apart from her lover, and their separation causes her to obsess over him.

Nature

The speaker compares her lover to a tree and her obsessive thoughts as vines which wrap around it. This imagery presents her love as something natural, but potentially uncontrollable if allowed to grow.

Obsession and control

The speaker obsesses over her lover and she can't think about anything else. However, she recognises her thoughts are no substitute for him, and she regains control of her obsession.

Form and structure

Sonnet 29 — 'I think of thee!' is a **sonnet**: a poetic form usually reserved for love poetry. Traditional sonnets tend to be about love from afar or unrequited love, and, initially, *Sonnet 29 — 'I think of thee!'* conforms to this expectation: the speaker is overwhelmed by thoughts of her lover while she is apart from him. However, the speaker subverts the expectation by choosing to be near her lover, rather than obsessing from afar.

Sonnets are usually categorised as **Shakespearean** or **Petrarchan**.

Comment: Shakespearean sonnets have 14 lines which are grouped into three **quatrains** (four rhyming lines) and end with a **rhyming couplet**. Petrarchan sonnets also have 14 lines, but they are made up of an octave (eight-line stanza) with an ABBAABBA rhyme scheme, followed by a sestet (six-line stanza) with either a CDCDCD or CDECDE rhyme scheme. The sestet usually begins with a **volta** (a turning point).

Sonnet 29 — 'I think of thee!' shares features with a Petrarchan sonnet but does not follow the form exactly. For example, the octave follows an ABBAABBA rhyme scheme, but the volta is on line 5 ("*Yet, O my palm-tree*") rather than line 9. Introducing the volta earlier in the poem could reflect the speaker's eagerness to be with her lover.

Comment: Another possibility is that the volta is on line 7: "*Rather, instantly*", as this signals when the speaker instructs her lover to overcome her obsessive thoughts.

The poem is written in the first person, and the speaker directly addresses her lover. This perspective creates a sense of intimacy.

Form and structure and continued

Enjambment in the first four lines mimics the fast and uncontrollable movement of the vine as it wraps around the tree. This shows how quickly the speaker is caught up in her obsessive thoughts.

The speaker uses **caesura** throughout the poem. This disrupts the rhythm which could reflect how her thoughts have become disjointed by her infatuation.

> **Comment:** The caesura also creates emphasis. For example, the dash before "*burst, shattered, everywhere!*" creates a dramatic pause which encourages the reader to focus on the urgent and dynamic phrase which follows. This is an important moment in the poem, as it symbolises the speaker breaking free from her obsessive thoughts.

The final line of the sonnet reverses the poem's first line: "*I think of thee!*" becomes "*I do not think of thee*". This change indicates that the speaker has taken control of her obsessive thoughts. This provides a satisfying conclusion for the reader, suggesting that the speaker will be happy now that she is close to her lover.

Tone

The poem has an intimate tone as it focuses on the speaker's adoration of her lover. As a reader, it feels almost intrusive reading such a personal poem.

> **Comment:** Barrett Browning did not intend for *Sonnet 29 — 'I think of thee!'* to be published, so the poem is likely to be an honest account of her personal feelings towards Robert.

The poem has an upbeat, positive tone. The speaker's love seems genuine and she anticipates the "*deep joy*" she will feel when she is with her lover again.

> **Comment:** The speaker's use of exclamation marks convey her excitement.

GCSE English Literature **Poetry Anthology** | Love and Relationships

Language

Extended metaphor

Throughout the poem the speaker uses an **extended metaphor** to compare her obsessive thoughts to vines that wrap around a tree. Like a vine, her thoughts keep growing until the tree is fully covered.

A palm tree.

Comment: Since Barrett Browning had been forbidden from marrying, she may have used plant imagery to present her feelings towards Robert as something natural and pure.

The speaker may have chosen to compare her lover to a "*palm-tree*" because palm trees grow for hundreds of years, suggesting that their love will endure for years to come. Palm trees can also survive in harsh climates, like deserts, suggesting that their forbidden love will also be able to survive the difficulties they face.

Comment: Palm trees are associated with Christianity (people waved palm branches as Jesus entered Jerusalem). This reinforces the idea that their love is pure and godly.

Representation of the speaker

Obsessive

The speaker acknowledges her thoughts are "*wild*", reinforcing that they are uncontrollable. She describes the vines as "*straggling*" which suggests her thoughts are inferior to the reality of his presence.

Comment: Barrett Browning may have used the word "*straggling*" in reference to her own ill health.

The speaker uses the possessive pronoun "*my*" in the phrase "*my palm-tree*" which suggests that she feels as though he belongs to her.

Comment: Although the speaker is initially presented as obsessive, following the volta she overcomes her infatuation, and controls her thoughts when she is with her lover.

Sexual

There are hints of the speaker's sexual desires. Her thoughts "*twine*" around her lover, which could be a reference to her body wrapped around his, and she commands him to "*set thy trunk all bare*", hinting that she wants to see him bare chested. This suggests that their relationship isn't just idealised, formal and distant, it's also passionate and sexual.

Comment: In Victorian society, it would have been shocking for women to acknowledge their sexuality, so the speaker disguises her desires using metaphors.

Language continued

Representation of the speaker's lover

Comment: Only the speaker's voice is heard: the reader doesn't hear directly from her lover. This reinforces how her obsession overwhelms her when they are not together.

The speaker presents her lover positively, which helps the reader understand her strong feelings towards him.

Supportive

Vines need a tree for support, so the speaker could be suggesting that she depends on her lover.

Comment: Women in Victorian society were often seen as the 'weaker' sex, so it's unsurprising that the speaker compares herself to "*straggling*" vines, whilst her lover is presented as a "*strong tree*".

Powerful

The speaker suggests that the palm tree can "*Rustle*" its "*boughs*" to shake the vines off, suggesting it can easily overpower the vines.

The tree (and therefore her lover) is described as "*strong*". The speaker seems to admire her lover's power.

Comment: The speaker uses **sibilance** across lines 8–9 to mimic the rustling of the tree's branches as it shakes the vines loose. This helps the reader imagine the scene that the speaker has created.

Representation of the relationship

Intense

The vines wrap around the tree so there's "*nought to see*", suggesting that the speaker is unable to think about anything other than him. The vines also "*insphere*" and hide "*the wood*", suggesting that the speaker's thoughts obscure her lover's true nature.

Loving

The speaker feels "*deep joy*" when they are together, and she can breathe "*a new air*". This suggests that she feels happy and calm in his presence.

COMPARING *SONNET 29* — *'I THINK OF THEE!'*

Here's how *Sonnet 29* — *'I think of thee!'* could be compared to other poems.

 Remember, you can compare *Sonnet 29* — *'I think of thee!'* with any poem from the anthology as long as your response is supported with examples. The following examples suggest ways to compare the poems, but they are not complete answers.

Extended metaphor

Sonnet 29 — *'I think of thee!'* uses an extended metaphor of vines wrapping around a tree to convey the speaker's obsessive thoughts about her lover. The speaker's use of natural imagery presents their love as natural, and suggests that their relationship, like vines and trees, will grow and flourish. The speaker compares her lover to a "*palm-tree*". Palm trees grow for hundreds of years in harsh desert climates, so this suggests that he is a permanent part of her life, and isn't afraid of adversity in their relationship.

Climbing My Grandfather (see **page 122**) also uses an extended metaphor. In this poem, the speaker is a child who climbs up his grandfather and compares the journey to climbing a mountain. This metaphor could represent a child getting to know his grandfather. Like, *Sonnet 29* — *'I think of thee!'*, the speaker also uses natural imagery. The speaker compares his grandfather to a mountain, which suggests that the speaker's grandfather also represents stability and permanence.

Changing emotions

Sonnet 29 — *'I think of thee!'* explores a change within a romantic relationship. Initially, the speaker is obsessed by thoughts of her lover, comparing them to vines that wrap around a tree so that there's "*nought to see*". However, a volta on line 5 marks a turning point in the speaker's attitude. She recognises that her thoughts are no substitute for being with her lover, and she breaks free from her infatuation. The speaker signals this change by reversing the opening line: "*I think of thee!*" becomes "*I do not think of thee*", which confirms to the reader she has been able to overcome her obsessive thoughts, and creates a sense of optimism for a healthier relationship.

Winter Swans (see **page 106**) also examines changing emotions within a romantic relationship. At first, the speaker acknowledges that his relationship with his partner is strained, as the couple are "*silent and apart*". This tense relationship is reinforced by the "*two days of rain*", which could symbolise the tears that the couple have cried. Like *Sonnet 29* — *'I think of thee!'*, the poem also has a volta, signalled by the appearance of "*the swans*" on line 7. The couple watch the swans' mating ritual, and the swans' unity inspires the couple to reunite, symbolised by them holding hands. This gesture shows that they are no longer "*apart*", and the description of "*afternoon light*" creates a hopeful tone, suggesting that the couple will be able to overcome the difficulties in their relationship.

Compare how poets present strong feelings in romantic relationships in *Sonnet 29 — 'I think of thee!'* and in **one** other poem from Love and Relationships. [30 marks]

Your answer may include:

AO1 — show understanding of the poems

- Both 'Sonnet 29 — 'I think of thee!'' and 'Love's Philosophy' focus on strong romantic feelings. In 'Sonnet 29 — 'I think of thee!'', the speaker is overwhelmed by strong romantic feelings, but she recognises that her obsession is unhealthy and she controls her infatuation. In 'Love's Philosophy', the speaker tries to convince his lover to be intimate with him. However, the poem doesn't have a turning point, and the speaker is unable to break free from his desires.

AO2 — show understanding of the poets' language choices

- Both poets use natural imagery to represent romantic love. In 'Sonnet 29 — 'I think of thee!'', the speaker uses an extended metaphor of a vine wrapping itself around a tree to represent her obsessive thoughts about her lover. However, using natural imagery implies that their relationship is pure and natural. In 'Love's Philosophy', the speaker uses natural imagery to convey his feelings of desire. He uses examples of interconnectedness found in nature, such as "fountains mingle with the river". The speaker may have also used natural imagery to suggest that an intimate relationship would be natural, rather than sinful.

- Since sex outside of marriage was taboo in the 19th century, both poets allude to sex, rather than admitting to their sexual desire. The speaker in 'Sonnet 29 — 'I think of thee!'' describes how her thoughts "twine" about her lover, suggesting that she is wrapping herself around him in a sexual way. This is reinforced by the description of to her lover's "bare" "trunk", alluding to him being half-dressed. In 'Love's Philosophy', the speaker describes how the "sunlight clasps the earth". The word "clasps" has connotations of a couple in a passionate embrace, suggesting the speaker's sexual desire.

- In 'Sonnet 29 — 'I think of thee!'', the speaker is able to break free from her obsessive thoughts. This is signalled by a reversal of the opening line in the final line: "I do not think of thee". This gives the poem a satisfying ending as the speaker overcomes her infatuation. However, in 'Love's Philosophy', the poem ends with the rhetorical question "What are all these kisses worth, / If thou kiss not me?". This suggests the speaker has been unsuccessful in pursuing his lover, and his lack of progress is unsatisfying for the reader.

AO3 — relate the poems to the context

- Both Barrett Browning and Shelley were Romantic poets, and their poems include typical features of this literary movement. Romantic poets often drew inspiration from the natural world, and focused on the power of extreme emotion. Consequently, both speakers suggest that romantic relationships can be overwhelming and lead to obsession.

This answer should be marked in accordance with the levels-based mark scheme on page 134.

Make sure your answer to this question is in paragraphs and full sentences. Bullet points have been used in this example answer to suggest some information you could include.

We've included some quotes from *Love's Philosophy* (**page 18**) in this sample answer, but direct quotes from the comparison poem aren't essential; you can use paraphrased examples or summaries to demonstrate your understanding.

NEUTRAL TONES — THOMAS HARDY

The speaker and his lover stand still. This reflects how their relationship has stagnated. The poem begins in the past tense, suggesting that this is a memory.

Winter is often associated with darkness and lifelessness. This establishes the mournful tone of the poem.

There is little colour in the scene, which matches the poem's title as well as the miserable mood of the poem.

We stood by a pond that winter day,
And the sun was white, as though chidden of God,
And a few leaves lay on the starving sod;
  — They had fallen from an ash, and were grey.

The ground is personified as "starving". This could reflect how the speaker's relationship is also dying.

The assonance in the phrase "rove / Over" mimics the slow, bored movement of the lover's eyes.

5 Your eyes on me were as eyes that rove
  Over tedious riddles of years ago;
  And some words played between us to and fro
    On which lost the more by our love.

"tedious" means 'boring'. This suggests that the speaker's partner has lost interest in him.

Some people thought crows and ravens were bad omens. The speaker suggests his lover's smile is a warning of things to come.

  The smile on your mouth was the deadest thing
10 Alive enough to have strength to die;
  And a grin of bitterness swept thereby
    Like an ominous bird a-wing...

This suggests that there is no warmth or love in the smile, which is an extension of how the speaker's partner feels about the relationship.

The final stanza fastforwards to the present. The speaker reflects that whenever he thinks of deceit, he recalls that meeting.

  Since then, keen lessons that love deceives,
  And wrings with wrong, have shaped to me
15 Your face, and the God curst sun, and a tree,
  And a pond edged with greyish leaves.

"God curst" is stronger than the phrase "chidden of God" on line 2. This suggests that the speaker has become more bitter over time.

The final line echoes the poem's opening. This cyclical structure hints that the speaker cannot escape the hurt caused by the relationship.

? **chidden of** — scolded by **sod** — soil
  a-wing — flying

Thomas Hardy

Thomas Hardy (1840–1928) was an English novelist and poet. Hardy was unlucky in love, and *Neutral Tones* conveys his cynicism and negativity towards romantic relationships. *Neutral Tones* was written in 1867, but it wasn't published until 1898 in his collection Wessex Poems. Hardy's work was influenced by the **Naturalism** movement (see below).

Thomas Hardy

Comment: The title *Neutral Tones* could reflect the colourless scene described in the poem, with its *"white sun"* and *"grey"* leaves. However, 'neutrality' can also mean 'not having a strong feeling towards something'. This could imply that the speaker's lover ended the relationship because she no longer had romantic feelings for him.

Summary of the poem

The speaker recalls standing with his lover by a pond on a winter's day. Their relationship is strained: the speaker's partner seems bored, and her expression suggests she has no affection towards him. The poem shifts to the present-day, and the speaker reflects on the meeting, and whenever he thinks of a deceitful relationship, he recalls that day by the pond.

Context and references

Naturalism was a literary movement that emerged in the 19th century. Naturalistic literature often included:

- **Realistic descriptions:** Naturalism focused on real life (rather than the supernatural), and everyday activities.
- **Pessimistic tone:** Naturalism often focused on life's difficulties.
- **Determinism:** Characters in Naturalistic literature were presented as having little control over their fate. Instead, a person's fate was believed to be predetermined, often influenced by their social class.

Comment: Naturalism rejected the overly emotional and sentimental themes found in Romantic literature (see **page 11**).

Themes

Loss and heartbreak
The poem focuses on a dying relationship. The speaker is angry and bitter, and he seems unable to forgive and move on.

Nature
Usually, nature represents growth and beauty, but in *Neutral Tones*, natural imagery is associated with death. The ground is "*starving*" and the leaves are "*grey*".

Death
The speaker includes multiple references to things that are dead or dying (see **page 45**). This mirrors the death of the couple's relationship and suggests that they won't be able to reconcile.

Distance
The couple have grown apart, and have become emotionally distant. The poem also includes temporal (time) distance: the break-up occurred in the past, but the speaker is still affected by it in the present.

Form and structure

Neutral Tones shares some similarities with an **elegy**: a type of poem written to commemorate the dead. Elegies often focused on feelings of grief and reflection.

Comment: Elegies were popular in the 18th century and were typically written in **quatrains** (4-line stanzas) with an ABAB rhyme scheme. Although *Neutral Tones* is structured in quatrains, it uses an ABBA rhyme scheme.

The regular ABBA rhyme scheme suggests that, although the speaker is bitter and resentful, he is in control of his emotions.

The poem is written in the first person, and is addressed to the speaker's former lover, using the second person "*your*". Addressing the poem to his ex-lover implies that the speaker still feels bitter about the relationship ending and blames her for his unhappiness.

The final line of each stanza is indented. This creates a pause and slows the pace of the poem, which mirrors the speaker's reflective and mournful tone.

The first three stanzas recall an unhappy memory by a pond when the couple's relationship was strained. The final stanza jumps forward in time. The speaker comments that he has had several relationships since, but he is still haunted by the memory of the day at the pond. This **cyclical** structure emphasises the effect that the memory has had on the speaker's life and suggests that he is stuck in the past and unable to move on, which is unsatisfying for the reader.

Tone

The poem has a pessimistic tone. There's no suggestion of hope or optimism: everything is colourless and devoid of life, and there's no indication the speaker has found happiness since the relationship ended.

Comment: A pessimistic tone was a feature of Naturalistic literature, and was a recurring theme in Hardy's poems and novels.

The poem also has a resentful tone. The speaker seems to blame his former lover for his subsequent unhappiness.

Language

Lifeless imagery

Throughout the poem, there are repeated references to death and lifelessness. This contributes to the pessimistic tone and reflects how the couple's relationship has died, with no hope that they will rekindle their love.

Comment: The imagery of death also mirrors the poem's form as an elegy.

- The poem starts in "*winter*", a cold season at the end of the year. This mirrors the coldness between the couple, and how their relationship is ending.
- The "*leaves lay*" motionless on the ground. Leaves that have fallen from trees are dead, and the **alliteration** adds to the sense of lifelessness.
- The ground is described as "*the starving sod*". The **personification** suggests that the ground is suffering, reinforced by **sibilance** which creates a gasping sound. This reflects how the couple's relationship is dying.
- The reference to "*ash*" suggests a fire that has burnt out and died. This represents how the warmth and affection shared by the couple has been replaced by coldness.
- His lover's smile is described as "*the deadest thing / Alive enough to have the strength to die*". This description implies there is no warmth or kindness in his lover's expression.

Comment: The couple also seem lifeless. They stand by the pond and do not move or speak to one another.

GCSE English Literature Poetry Anthology | *Love and Relationships*

Language continued

Subversion of typical romance poetry

The speaker refers to his former lover's "*eyes*" and "*smile*", body parts that are frequently romanticised in love poetry and are often used show a person's happiness. However, the speaker subverts this by describing how his lover's eyes reveal her boredom, using **assonance** in the phrase "*rove / Over*" to mimic the slow, bored movement of her eyes. His lover's smile is described as the "*deadest thing*". The **superlative** (an adjective which indicates something is the 'most', usually signalled by the ending -est) reinforces just how cold and lifeless her smile is.

His lover's smile is also described as "*an ominous bird a-wing*". Usually, birds are used to symbolise hope and freedom, but in this example, the image of a bird flying away could symbolise the end of their relationship.

> **Comment:** Some birds (such as crows and ravens) were thought to warn people of bad things to come. The speaker sees his lover's bitter smile as an "*ominous*" sign that their relationship is ending.

Colourless language

The title *Neutral Tones* accurately describes the colourless setting. The "*sun*", usually associated with gold and yellow, is "*white*". The leaves, usually associated with green, or orange in autumn, are "*grey*" and "*greyish*". All colour has been sapped from the scene, which reflects how the vibrancy has disappeared from their relationship.

Religious language

The speaker describes the sun as "*chidden by God*" in the first stanza and "*God-curst*" in the final stanza. Usually, God is associated with forgiveness and compassion, so presenting God as hostile suggests that the speaker cannot even find comfort in religion. This reinforces the hopeless tone and overwhelming negativity of the speaker.

> **Comment:** The phrases "*chidden by God*" and "*God curst*" could also suggest that God disapproves of their relationship and it was doomed to fail.

Language continued

Representation of the speaker

Complicated

The speaker compares himself to "*tedious riddles*". This suggests that his partner has grown bored of his complicated personality.

Comment: The semantic field of riddles and games is reinforced by the words "*played*", "*to and fro*" and "*lost*". This suggests that the couple's relationship wasn't easy or straightforward, and that they tried to confuse each other with mind games.

Cynical

The speaker believes that "*love deceives*". This generalisation suggests that the heartbreak the speaker experienced has made him cynical about love.

Comment: The speaker has learnt "*keen lessons*" about the deceptive nature of love. The word "*keen*" can mean 'sharp'. This suggests that his experiences with love have been painful.

Representation of the ex-lover

Deceptive

The speaker's comment that "*love deceives*" could hint that his lover betrayed him in some way.

Comment: The reader doesn't hear from the ex-lover directly or learn what caused the breakdown in the relationship. The reader only learns about the ex-lover through the speaker, and his perceptions may be biased or unreliable.

Resentful

The speaker's former partner has a "*grin of bitterness*". This **oxymoron** suggests that she is trying to mask her feelings, but she cannot disguise the resentment she feels.

COMPARING *NEUTRAL TONES*

Here's how *Neutral Tones* could be compared to other poems.

 Remember, you can compare *Neutral Tones* with any poem from the anthology as long as your response is supported with examples. The following examples suggest ways to compare the poems, but they are not complete answers.

Unhappy memories

Neutral Tones focuses on an unhappy memory which has influenced the speaker in later life. The speaker describes a painful break-up which has haunted him for many years, and the cyclical structure (referencing the meeting by the "*pond*" in both the first and final stanzas) suggests that he is stuck in the past and cannot move on. The memory is also significant because it changed the speaker's outlook on love and romantic relationships. The final stanza jumps forward in time to the present, where the speaker comments that "*love deceives*". This generalisation suggests that the end of this relationship made him cynical and pessimistic towards love.

Follower (see **page 82**) examines a parental relationship rather than a romantic relationship, but the speaker also explores unhappy memories which have impacted his outlook in the present. The speaker admires his father's skill as a farmer, calling him "*An expert*", however, the speaker recognises that he was unable to live up to his father's abilities. This is reflected in the image of the speaker stumbling in his father's "*hob-nailed wake*", which suggests that the speaker wanted to follow in his father's footsteps, but the verb "*stumbling*" implies he was unsuccessful. The final stanza also jumps forward in time to the present, and the speaker's failure to live up to his father's expectations have created conflict in their relationship. The speaker feels resentful towards his father, commenting that he "*will not go away*".

Personification

Neutral Tones uses personification to reflect the unhappy tone of the poem. The speaker describes the "*starving sod*", and the sibilance in this phrase creates an unpleasant hissing sound, which draws attention to the personification. The word "*starving*" suggests the ground is suffering through lack of attention, which reflects how the couple's relationship is also dying. This description in the first stanza creates a miserable mood which continues throughout the reminder of the poem.

Porphyria's Lover (see **pages 26–27**) also uses personification to establish the mood of the poem, however, this mood is unsettling and threatening, rather than miserable. The speaker describes the "*sullen wind*" which "*tore the elm-tops down for spite*" and "*did its worst to vex the lake*". This presents the wind as an antagonistic and vicious, deliberately harming the trees and lake. This foreshadows the speaker's violent behaviour later in the poem.

Compare how poets present difficult relationships in *Neutral Tones* and in **one** other poem from Love and Relationships.

[30 marks]

Your answer may include:

AO1 — show understanding of the poems

- Both 'Neutral Tones' and 'Winter Swans' explore strained relationships where the couples are drifting apart. In 'Neutral Tones', the speaker describes the end of a relationship, and how the break-up has left him resentful and bitter. However, although the couple in 'Winter Swans' initially appear to be drifting apart, they reconcile after watching a pair of swans on a lake.

AO2 — show understanding of the poets' language choices

- Both 'Neutral Tones' and 'Winter Swans' use descriptions of the weather to reinforce the mood of the poem. In 'Neutral Tones', the couple meet on a "winter day", implying that it is cold and uncomfortable, just like the couple's relationship. In 'Winter Swans', it has been raining for "two days". Rain often has connotations of sadness and despair, which matches the unhappiness of the couple.

- Both poems establish the tension and growing distance felt by the couples. In 'Neutral Tones', the lover's smile is described as the "deadest thing". This metaphor suggests that there is no affection or warmth behind her expression, and that the relationship is strained. In 'Winter Swans', the couple are described as "silent and apart", suggesting the emotional distance between them, and their inability to communicate with each other.

- Although both poems focus on difficult relationships, they have different endings. In 'Neutral Tones', the couple are unable to repair their relationship, and their break-up has a lasting impact on the speaker, who cynically declares that "love deceives". This creates a pessimistic ending which suggests that being in love only ends in misery and hopelessness. However, in 'Winter Swans', the couple eventually reconcile, and the poem ends with them holding hands, symbolising how they have reconnected and overcome the emotional distance between them. This ending is optimistic and suggests that love can be challenging, but it is worth fighting for.

AO3 — relate the poems to the context

- Both poems suggest that romantic love can cause pain and unhappiness. 'Winter Swans' implies that couples can overcome difficulties, however, 'Neutral Tones' warns that unhappy romantic relationships can taint a person's outlook, and make them cynical towards love.

This answer should be marked in accordance with the levels-based mark scheme on page 134.

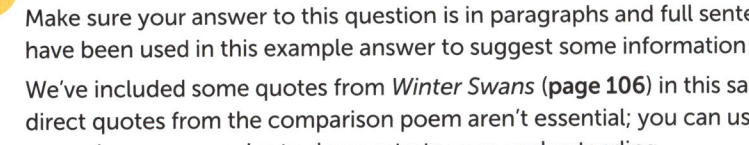

Make sure your answer to this question is in paragraphs and full sentences. Bullet points have been used in this example answer to suggest some information you could include.

We've included some quotes from *Winter Swans* (**page 106**) in this sample answer, but direct quotes from the comparison poem aren't essential; you can use paraphrased examples or summaries to demonstrate your understanding.

THE FARMER'S BRIDE — CHARLOTTE MEW

The farmer "*chose*" his wife, suggesting the marriage may not have been a mutual decision and that he has the power in the relationship.

"*maid*" often refers to a woman who is a virgin, so this highlights her youth and inexperience.

The bride only became afraid after marriage. This could suggest a fear of sexual intimacy.

This simile describes the coldness between the couple.

This line is longer than the others and mimics the breathlessness of the villagers as they chase her.

The wife is hunted and captured like an animal. The farmer has gathered other local people which makes the chase seem more intimidating.

This simile compares the bride to a mouse, suggesting that she is timid, but also prey for larger animals.

This reinforces the expectation placed on her to be sexually intimate with her husband. Instead, she lies awake, which suggests she fears he may try to touch her in her sleep.

The farmer doesn't attempt to comfort her or understand why she ran away. He just locks the doors to prevent her from escaping again.

This emphasises how she feels safe and comfortable around small animals, but also reminds the reader of her youth: "*chat and play*" mimics childlike behaviour.

The bride is voiceless throughout the poem. This reflects her silence in the relationship, but also how she is powerless.

Three Summers since I chose a maid,
Too young maybe — but more's to do
    At harvest-time than bide and woo.
    When us was wed she turned afraid
5   Of love and me and all things human;
Like the shut of a winter's day
Her smile went out, and 'twadn't a woman —
    More like a little frightened fay.
        One night, in the Fall, she runned away.

10 "Out 'mong the sheep, her be," they said,
'Should properly have been abed;
But sure enough she wadn't there
Lying awake with her wide brown stare.
So over seven-acre field and up-along across the down
15 We chased her, flying like a hare
    Before our lanterns. To Church-Town
All in a shiver and a scare
We caught her, fetched her home at last
And turned the key upon her, fast.

20 She does the work about the house
As well as most, but like a mouse:
Happy enough to chat and play
    With birds and rabbits and such as they,
    So long as men-folk keep away.
25 "Not near, not near!" her eyes beseech
    When one of us comes within reach.
        The women say that beasts in stall
        Look round like children at her call.
I've hardly heard her speak at all.

| This description suggests that she is physically undeveloped, reminding the reader of her youth. | | The speaker compares his wife to animals and plants. This reinforces her as something wild and untameable. |

30   Shy as a leveret, swift as he,
     Straight and slight as a young larch tree,
     Sweet as the first wild violets, she,
     To her wild self. But what to me?

     The short days shorten and the oaks are brown,
35   The blue smoke rises to the low grey sky,
     One leaf in the still air falls slowly down,
         A magpie's spotted feathers lie
     On the black earth spread white with rime,
     The berries redden up to Christmas-time.
40   What's Christmas-time without there be
     Some other in the house than we!

         She sleeps up in the attic there
     Alone, poor maid. 'Tis but a stair
     Betwixt us. Oh! my God! the down,
45   The soft young down of her, the brown,
     The brown of her — her eyes, her hair, her hair!

| This could represent the isolation felt by both the farmer and the bride. |
| The farmer longs for a child. |
| This speaker uses a sarcastic tone. The bride is probably very happy alone. |
| Describing the hair on her as "*young down*" reinforces the image of the bride as a baby animal. |
| The rhetorical question suggests the speaker's resentment towards his wife. He feels that his wife owes him affection. |
| This implies that the bride no longer sleeps in the same bed as her husband, and their lives are separate. |
| "*maid*" suggests that she is still a virgin and they haven't consummated their marriage. |
| The repetition of "*her*" indicates the speaker's obsession with his wife. |
| The use of exclamation marks shows the speaker's overwhelming desire for his wife. |
| The increased use of caesura in the final stanza suggests the farmer struggles to concentrate as he is overwhelmed by desire. |

? **bide** — stay **woo** — pursue romantically **fay** — fairy **beseech** — ask
  leveret — young hare **rime** — frost **down** — fine, soft hair

GCSE English Literature Poetry Anthology | Love and Relationships   51

Charlotte Mew

Charlotte Mew (1869–1928) was an English poet. She wrote *The Farmer's Bride* in 1916.

Charlotte Mew

Summary of the poem

A farmer recalls marrying his wife three years earlier, even though she was too young to be married. She was unhappy in the relationship, so she ran away. Local people chased her and brought her back to the farmer. The farmer now keeps his wife locked inside where she does the housework. She will talk to animals and other women, but seems afraid of men, and refuses to talk to them. The farmer longs for a child, but his wife sleeps alone. The poem ends with the farmer lusting after his wife.

Context and references

Marriage in the early 20th century

At the turn of the 20th century, society was patriarchal, and women had much less power than men. Women 'belonged' to their fathers, and once they were married, they 'belonged' to their husbands.

Comment: In the poem, the bride is so unhappy she runs away. Rather than let her go, the farmer captures her and locks her up. This suggests that the farmer feels he 'owns' his wife.

At the time, marriages were primarily viewed as business proposals, and a couple could only marry if their families approved of the match. In the early 20th century, the farmer would have been a catch since he owned land and could offer a wife financial security. It's likely that the farmer would have had his pick of the local women, as parents would have been keen for him to marry their daughter.

Reaction to poem

Readers' responses to the characters may have changed since the poem was written over 100 years ago. Readers in the early 20th century may have sympathised with the farmer: he works hard to provide for his bride, and he is lonely because she offers little companionship. By early 20th century standards, the farmer does not treat his wife unkindly as he does not physically abuse her. Readers may have criticised the bride, as she has not fulfilled her 'duties' by consummating the marriage and providing him with children.

Comment: When *The Farmer's Bride* was written, some people were speaking out against gender inequality. Mew may have written the poem to show how a patriarchal society affected women.

However, modern audiences are more likely to sympathise with the bride: she was unwillingly married at a young age to man who showed little interest in their compatibility. He has locked her in his home where she is expected to do household chores, and despite her obvious unhappiness, he is unwilling to free her from the relationship. Modern readers may also feel unsettled by the poem's ending, and the implication that the farmer may rape his wife.

Themes

Romantic love
The poem focuses on a strained relationship between a farmer and his wife.

Nature
The poem has a rural setting, and the speaker compares the bride to plants and animals (see **page 55**).

Distance
Although the farmer and his bride live in the same house, they are emotionally distant.

Obsession and control
The speaker tries to control his bride by locking her up after she runs away. In the final stanza, the farmer hints at his obsessive desire for his wife.

Form and structure

The poem is a **dramatic monologue** told in the first person from the perspective of the farmer. His bride remains voiceless throughout, which shows her powerlessness and the control the farmer has over her.

The poem is made up of six stanzas of unequal length, and the rhyme scheme and length of the stanzas change to match the pace of the story. For example, the second stanza focuses on the bride's escape and subsequent capture. The pace of this stanza mimics the frenzy and urgency of the chase: line 14 has more syllables than the lines before or after which mimics the breathlessness of the group as they chase the bride. The final stanza focuses on the farmer's desire for his bride. His lust is reinforced by **caesura**, which creates a choppy, disjointed rhythm which implies he cannot concentrate because he is overwhelmed by desire. The use of **enjambment** reinforces his lust, as it suggests he cannot control his racing thoughts.

> **Comment:** The poem's irregular rhyme scheme could mimic the ineloquent nature of the farmer. As someone who spends a lot of time alone, he may struggle to express himself.

Tone

The poem has a miserable tone. Both the farmer and the bride are trapped in an unhappy marriage.

> **Comment:** When the poem was written, divorce was socially unacceptable, so unhappy couples often stayed together.

The poem also has a frustrated tone. The farmer's bride does not satisfy him emotionally or physically.

Language

Language of ownership

The title, *The Farmer's Bride*, implies that the farmer owns his wife. The bride's name is never revealed, so she isn't given an identity beyond 'belonging' to the farmer.

The farmer "*chose*" his bride, which implies that their marriage wasn't a mutual decision. The verb "*chose*" also suggests that the farmer picked her like livestock at market.

When the bride runs away and is brought back to the farm, the farmer imprisons her. Rather than try to comfort her or understand why she has run away, he locks her up like an escaped animal. This suggests he sees her as something he possesses, rather than cares for.

Representation of the farmer

Rural

The speaker uses non-standard grammar and spelling which represents his accent and dialect, for example, "*When us was wed*" and "*she runned away*". In the early 20th century, non-standard language was commonly used by people in rural areas, so this gives the farmer a believable voice.

The speaker measures time using the seasons. For example, "*Three Summers since*", "*harvest-time*" and "*in the Fall*" (autumn) which reflects his job as a farmer who needs be attuned to the changing weather.

Comment: The seasons also match the couple's changing relationship. They get together in summer, a season associated with warmth and happiness, but the bride runs away during autumn. Autumn marks the beginning of shorter, darker days, symbolising the bride's unhappiness. The end of the poem is set during "*Christmas-time*" (winter), a season associated with cold temperatures and darkness, and this reflects the coldness between the couple. Winter is also a time when nothing grows, which reinforces how the couple are childless.

Practical

The farmer acknowledges that working on the farm was more important than getting to know his wife-to-be: "*more's to do / At harvest-time than bide and woo*". This suggests he prioritised the farm over their relationship.

Frustrated

The farmer is disappointed and frustrated that he doesn't have a relationship with his wife ("*But what to me?*") and he longs to have children.

The final stanza reveals the farmer's sexual frustration. The repeated use of "*her*" across lines 45–46 shows how his thoughts are consumed by his bride, and the use of exclamation marks across lines 44–46 show the strength of his feelings. He objectifies his bride by focusing on her physical features, including her "*eyes*" and "*hair*".

Language continued

Representation of the bride

Vulnerable

The speaker uses **zoomorphism** (figurative language where humans are given animal qualities) to compare the bride to animals throughout the poem, for example, "*hare*", "*mouse*" and "*leveret*". These are all small prey animals, which are hunted by larger predators. This reinforces the bride's vulnerability and powerlessness.

Comment: Comparing the bride to animals also reinforces the speaker's rural upbringing.

When the bride escapes, the local people "*chased*" and "*caught*" her, which reminds the reader of a wild animal being hunted.

Young

The poem also emphasises the bride's youth. The speaker suggests she was "*Too young*" to marry, and this is reinforced by her being described as "*straight and slight*", implying that she was physically undeveloped. This creates sympathy from the reader.

The bride prefers to "*chat and play*" with animals. These childish verbs remind the reader of her youth, implying that she isn't mature enough to be a wife and mother.

Fearful

When the bride marries the farmer, "*she turned afraid / Of love*". This hints that the bride was afraid when the farmer attempted to consummate the marriage.

Comment: Women in the early 20th century were expected to be virgins when they married, and often had very little knowledge of sex. The farmer may have attempted to have sex with the bride, which frightened her. She is referred to as a "*bride*" and a "*maid*" (virgin) rather than a 'wife' implying that they have not consummated the marriage.

The bride's fear continues throughout the poem, and she is described as "*frightened*" and "*a scare*". This makes the marriage seem torturous as she lives in constant fear.

Dutiful

The farmer admits that the bride "*does the work about the house / As well as most*", suggesting that she is a dutiful housewife. However, it was also a woman's 'duty' to have children: something she is unwilling to do.

Silent

We only hear the farmer's voice in the poem: the bride never speaks which reflects her silence towards her husband and her powerlessness in the relationship. The farmer admits that he's "*hardly heard her speak at all*".

COMPARING *THE FARMER'S BRIDE*

Here's how *The Farmer's Bride* could be compared to other poems.

Remember, you can compare *The Farmer's Bride* with any poem from the anthology as long as your response is supported with examples. The following examples suggest ways to compare the poems, but they are not complete answers.

Obsession

The speaker in *The Farmer's Bride* is presented as being obsessed with his wife. In the final stanza, the speaker repeatedly uses exclamation marks when speaking about his bride, for example, "*her hair!*", which conveys his strong feelings towards her. The exclamation marks, along with other pieces of punctuation, also create caesura in the poem. These pauses create a choppy, disjointed rhythm, which suggest that the speaker cannot control his racing thoughts about his wife. The final line repeats the word "*her*" four times, which suggests he is overwhelmed by his obsession.

The speaker in *Sonnet 29 — 'I think of thee!'* (see **page 34**) is also presented as being obsessed with her lover, and she also uses exclamation marks to show her infatuation, for example, the opening phrase "*I think of thee!*". The speaker also uses caesura throughout the poem, and this disjointed rhythm emphasises how she is overwhelmed by her obsessive thoughts. However, unlike the farmer, the speaker in *Sonnet 29 — 'I think of thee!'* regains control by being in the presence of her lover.

Cold language

The speaker in *The Farmer's Bride* uses language associated with coldness to present his relationship with his wife. He uses the simile "*Like the shut of a winter's day*" to describe how she rejected him after their wedding. The word "*shut*" implies that she has become closed off and distant, and the phrase "*winter's day*" suggests she is behaving coldly and there is no warmth or affection between them. This simile is used in the first stanza, which sets the tone for their relationship, and introduces the marital difficulties between the speaker and his wife.

The speaker in *When We Two Parted* (see **page 10**) also refers to coldness when describing his ex-lover. He describes her cheek as "*cold*" and her kiss as "*Colder*". The speaker interprets his partner's coldness as a sign of their struggling relationship. Like the speaker in *The Farmer's Bride*, the speaker in *When We Two Parted* introduces his lover's coldness in the first stanza, which establishes the struggling nature of the relationship early in the poem.

Compare how poets present ideas about controlling relationships in *The Farmer's Bride* and in **one** other poem from Love and Relationships. [30 marks]

Your answer may include:

AO1 — show understanding of the poems

- Both 'The Farmer's Bride' and 'Porphyria's Lover' explore control, and the balance of power in relationships. In 'The Farmer's Bride', the speaker controls his wife by keeping her locked inside the house. In 'Porphyria's Lover', Porphyria initially seems to assert dominance over the speaker, however, this balance of power shifts when he murders Porphyria.

AO2 — show understanding of the poets' language choices

- Both poems are dramatic monologues from a male perspective. The voices of neither Porphyria nor the farmer's bride are heard in the poem. This voicelessness represents how women were often powerless in relationships in the 19th and early 20th century.
- Both speakers use language associated with control. In 'The Farmer's Bride', the speaker describes how he "chose a maid". This implies that the relationship was not a mutual decision, and establishes the farmer as the person with control in the relationship. In 'Porphyria's Lover', the speaker describes Porphyria as "mine, mine". The use of repetition reinforces how he believes he 'owns' Porphyria.
- Both speakers suggest they have control by emphasising their partners' small size. In 'The Farmer's Bride', the speaker compares his bride to a "hare" and a "mouse". These are small prey animals, which suggest her vulnerability. Similarly, the speaker in 'Porphyria's Lover', describes Porphyria's "little throat" and "little head". This suggests the speaker feels larger and more powerful than Porphyria. Both speakers see their partners as smaller and weaker, which allows them to physically control them. In 'The Farmer's Bride', this control is shown when the farmer locks his bride in the house, and in 'Porphyria's Lover' when the speaker murders Porphyria.

AO3 — relate the poems to the context

- When these poems were written, society was patriarchal and women were believed to 'belong' to their father or their husbands. The concept of men owning and controlling women in relationships was much more widespread and accepted than it is today.
- Both Mew and Browning believed that women should have more rights. They may have wanted their poems to highlight the inequality women faced in the 19th and early 20th centuries by showing the destructive nature of controlling relationships, and the unhappiness they cause.

This answer should be marked in accordance with the levels-based mark scheme on page 134.

Make sure your answer to this question is in paragraphs and full sentences. Bullet points have been used in this example answer to suggest some information you could include.

We've included some quotes from *Porphyria's Lover* (**page 30**) in this sample answer, but direct quotes from the comparison poem aren't essential; you can use paraphrased examples or summaries to demonstrate your understanding.

WALKING AWAY — CECIL DAY-LEWIS

This symbolises the new boundaries that have been created between father and son.

A lot of time has passed but the memory is still clear. This shows the impact that it has had on the speaker's life.

The seasonal change from summer to autumn echoes the emotional change between father and son.

This presents the speaker as an observer. He can no longer control his child's future, instead he can only watch.

It is eighteen years ago, almost to the day –
A sunny day with leaves just turning,
The touch-lines new-ruled – since I watched you play
Your first game of football, then, like a satellite
5   Wrenched from its orbit, go drifting away

"Wrenched" suggests that the separation was painful.

Satellites are far from Earth, so this simile reinforces the distance between the father and son.

The speaker compares his son's future to a "wilderness" which has connotations of adventure, but also danger.

Behind a scatter of boys. I can see
You walking away from me towards the school
With the pathos of a half-fledged thing set free
Into a wilderness, the gait of one
10 Who finds no path where the path should be.

"away" is repeated throughout, which reinforces the theme of separation.

That hesitant figure, eddying away
Like a winged seed loosened from its parent stem,
Has something I never quite grasp to convey
About nature's give-and-take – the small, the scorching
15 Ordeals which fire one's irresolute clay.

Clay is soft until it is fired in a kiln, where the heat hardens it. The speaker likens emotional "Ordeals" to the heat of a kiln which makes someone stronger.

"Gnaws" is an unpleasant word which suggests that the memory is painful for the speaker.

I have had worse partings, but none that so
Gnaws at my mind still. Perhaps it is roughly
Saying what God alone could perfectly show –
How selfhood begins with a walking away,
20 And love is proved in the letting go.

The speaker reassures himself that letting his son gain his own independence is a way of showing his love as a father.

This line could refer to both the father and the son. They both accept that they need to let the other walk away.

> **?**   **pathos** — something that makes you feel sad
> **gait** — the way that someone walks
> **eddying** — water or air moving in a circular motion
> **gnaws** — nibbles (usually associated with animals)

Cecil Day-Lewis

Cecil Day-Lewis (1904–1972) was an Irish-born poet. His mother died when he was two, so Day-Lewis was raised by his father. The importance of father-son relationships is examined in *Walking Away*, which was first published in 1962. Day-Lewis became **Poet Laureate** in 1968.

Poet Laureate is an honorary position appointed by the King or Queen of the United Kingdom. There are few specific duties, but the poet is expected to write poems for significant national events.

Cecil Day-Lewis

Summary of the poem

A father reminisces about watching his son play a school football match eighteen years ago. After the game ends, the son walks away from the speaker, which makes him feel sad because his son is becoming more independent, and no longer needs him. In the final stanza, the speaker acknowledges the impact that the memory has had on him, and that letting his son go was a way to prove his love.

Context and references

Sean Day-Lewis

The poem is about Day-Lewis's son, Sean, who was sent to boarding school aged seven.

Since Day-Lewis had a close relationship with his own father, the poem could hint at the regret he feels at sending his son to boarding school, rather than developing a parental relationship at home.

Comment: The poem was originally subtitled *"for Sean"*.

Themes

Loss and heartbreak
The father finds his son's growing independence difficult, because he worries about his son's safety.

Family relationships
The poem examines the changing relationship between a father and son as the son grows up and becomes more independent.

Nature
The speaker uses natural imagery (see **page 62**) to describe his feelings towards his son becoming more independent.

Distance
The poem focuses on the physical and emotional distance between father and son.

Form and structure

The poem is written in the first person, from the perspective of a father speaking to his son. This creates a sense of intimacy, as the reader experiences something personal to the speaker.

Comment: It's likely that the speaker of the poem is the poet reflecting on an event that actually happened, so this poem is **autobiographical**.

The poem is made up of four stanzas with five lines each. The lines have a regular ABACA rhyme scheme. The 'A' rhyme could reflect how the speaker is reminded about the memory of that day. The 'B' and 'C' lines could reflect how the son wants to break free from his father.

The speaker uses **caesura** throughout the poem. This could represent the speaker's hesitancy to let his son go, but also the son's hesitancy to become independent from his father.

The poem reflects on an event which happened "*eighteen*" years ago. This reinforces how significant this memory was to the speaker, and how he still thinks about it almost two decades later.

Comment: The poem has a satisfying conclusion, as the speaker accepts that he did the right thing, even though letting go of his son was painful. The poem may offer reassurance for any parent faced with a similar situation.

Tone

The poem has a sentimental tone. It describes an emotionally significant day for both the speaker and the son.

The speaker's tone is conflicted. He doubts his son is old enough to be independent, and he worries about his son's safety. However, he also accepts that it is inevitable that most children become less reliant on their parents as they grow up.

Language

Language of change

The speaker uses imagery related to change to represent his relationship with his son.

The speaker describes a "*day with the leaves just turning*", which implies that the events of the poem occur on the cusp of autumn. This changing season mirrors how the son is growing up and moving on to the next season of his life. Like the changing of the seasons, the son's desire for independence is also inevitable.

Comment: Autumn is associated with colder weather and darker days hinting that the father will find his son's growing independence difficult.

The "*touch lines new-ruled*" describes fresh pitch markings on the football field. However, this also implies new boundaries being established between father and son. For example, older children are often given more freedom, such as later curfews and more time spent apart from their parents.

The phrase "*scorching / Ordeals that fire one's irresolute clay*" compares soft clay being hardened in a kiln to a young person being hardened by difficult experiences. The speaker acknowledges that his son will face hardships as he gets older, but these situations will make him stronger and more resilient.

Comment: Clay is malleable (its shape can be changed). Comparing his son to clay could suggest that other people may influence his son and try to change him.

GCSE English Literature Poetry Anthology | Love and Relationships

Language continued

Natural imagery

The speaker uses natural imagery to describe his son growing up. Using examples from nature reinforces that growing up and gaining independence is a natural part of development.

The speaker compares his son to a *"half-fledged thing set free / Into a wilderness"*. The phrase *"half-fledged"* describes a bird that is learning to fly but isn't quite strong enough. This suggests the speaker is concerned his son isn't mature enough to be independent. The phrase *"set free / Into a wilderness"* suggests that the speaker's son is on the verge of freedom and adventure, but also danger and potential loneliness.

The **simile** *"Like a winged seed loosened from its parent stem"* describes the son as a *"seed"* which suggests his potential to grow and develop into something much bigger. The word *"winged"* has connotations of flying away and freedom, and the word *"loosened"* suggests that the separation between father and son was gentle.

> **Comment:** The example of a *"winged seed"* also suggests that the separation from the *"parent stem"* is irreversible, and that the change in the pair's relationship is permanent.

Language of separation

The speaker repeats phrases linked to separation. He describes his son as *"drifting away"*, *"walking away"* and *"eddying away"*. The verbs suggest that the separation is slow and gradual, which reflects how children gaining their independence is a gradual process too.

Representation of the speaker's son

Uncertain

The speaker describes his son as a *"hesitant figure"*, suggesting his uncertainty. The son's hesitancy helps the reader understand why the speaker finds the experience so difficult: the speaker is worried whether his son will be able to succeed on his own, and he is concerned for his son's safety.

Language continued

Representation of the speaker

Passive

The speaker can only watch as his son walks away from him. Although it is painful for the speaker, he acknowledges he cannot stop his son from becoming independent.

Upset

The speaker uses the vivid verbs "*Wrenched*" and "*Gnaws*" to describe his feelings towards his son becoming independent. The speaker's choice of language suggests that his son gaining independence was a painful experience.

Concerned

The speaker comments that his son "*finds no path where the path should be*". This suggests that the speaker is worried his son is still trying to find his place in the world. This lack of direction suggests that the speaker is concerned his son will follow the 'wrong' path.

The speaker is also worried his son will face "*Scorching / Ordeals*", suggesting that the son will face painful and unpleasant experiences as he grows up.

> **Comment:** Parents spend years protecting their children from harm. As children grow older, parents acknowledge that they must let their children make their own mistakes.

Accepting

In the final two lines, the speaker accepts that allowing his son freedom is the best way he can show his love.

COMPARING *WALKING AWAY*

Here's how *Walking Away* could be compared to other poems.

 Remember, you can compare *Walking Away* with any poem from the anthology as long as your response is supported with examples. The following examples suggest ways to compare the poems, but they are not complete answers.

Separation vs connection

Walking Away focuses on emotional and physical distance between a father and his adolescent son. This sense of separation is reinforced through the speaker's use of language, for example "*drifting away*", "*walking away*" and "*eddying away*". The verbs suggest the separation is gradual, which reflects the process of a child growing into an adolescent and slowly gaining more independence. The repetition of "*away*" emphasises the distance between the father the son.

On the other hand, *Climbing My Grandfather* (see **page 122**) focuses on a growing connection between a grandfather and his grandchild. This developing bond is shown through language from the semantic field of knowledge. At first, the speaker tries "*to get a grip*" on his grandfather, suggesting that he wants to learn more about him. As the poem progresses, the speaker "*discover[s]*" more about his grandfather. At the end of the poem, the speaker describes "*knowing*" his grandfather, which suggests he has connected with him and understands him.

Natural imagery

In *Walking Away*, the speaker uses natural imagery to describe the emotional and physical distance between a parent and a child as the child grows up. The speaker compares his son to a "*winged seed loosened from its parent stem*". This simile suggests that the separation from the "*parent stem*" is irreversible, and that the relationship between the father and son will be permanently changed. The word "*winged*" suggests that the son has gained his freedom, and may fly far away from his father. "*seed*" suggests the son has potential to grow and flourish as he becomes an adult.

In *Letters From Yorkshire* (see **page 66**), the speaker also uses natural imagery to describe a relationship between a parent and a child, however, unlike in *Walking Away*, the imagery emphasises the connection between the father and daughter, rather than separation. In the poem, the speaker uses the metaphor of her father "*pouring light and air into an envelope*". This suggests that the letters the speaker receives from her father are invigorating and uplifting, like sitting in sunshine and breathing fresh air. This conveys the closeness felt between the speaker and her father.

Compare how poets present parental relationships in *Walking Away* and in **one** other poem from Love and Relationships. [30 marks]

Your answer may include:

AO1 — show understanding of the poems

- Both 'Walking Away' and 'Before You Were Mine' explore relationships between parents and children. However, 'Walking Away' is written from the perspective of a father to his son, whereas 'Before You Were Mine' is written from the perspective of a daughter to a mother.
- Both poems focus on difficult experiences in parent-child relationships. In 'Walking Away', the speaker reflects on the pain caused by his son becoming older and gaining his independence. In 'Before You Were Mine', the speaker feels guilty about ending her mother's youth with the responsibility of being a parent.

AO2 — show understanding of the poets' language choices

- Both poems focus on past events and how these events have affected the speaker in the present. In 'Walking Away', the speaker describes a memory from "eighteen" years ago watching his son play football, and the pain he felt as his son walked away from him. This reinforces how emotionally significant the memory was for the speaker, and how it still "Gnaws" at his mind. The word "Gnaws" suggests the speaker feels regret or guilt about sending his son to boarding school. In 'Before You Were Mine', the speaker uses a photograph of her mother to imagine what she was like when she was younger. The speaker presents her mother's youth as carefree and lively ("you sparkle and waltz and laugh") but she acknowledges that this version of her mother became a "ghost" when she became a parent. The speaker feels guilty that her birth restricted her mother's freedom.
- Both speakers use imagery associated with walking along a path to symbolise life's journey. In 'Walking Away', the speaker is concerned because his son "finds no path where the path should be". This suggests that the son is uncertain about his direction in life, and the speaker is worried his son will follow the 'wrong' path. In 'Before You Were Mine', the speaker describes the potential that the "right walk home could bring", suggesting that her mother's life is full of promise. However, this changes in the final stanza, with a description of the "wrong pavement", suggesting that her mother made the wrong choices in life.

AO3 — relate the poems to the context

- Both poems are autobiographical and explore real relationships. 'Walking Away' is about Day-Lewis's son, Sean, and 'Before You Were Mine' is about Duffy's mother. This makes the feelings of longing and regret expressed in the poems more genuine and heartfelt, and suggests that relationships between parents and children can sometimes be painful and difficult.

This answer should be marked in accordance with the levels-based mark scheme on page 134.

Make sure your answer to this question is in paragraphs and full sentences. Bullet points have been used in this example answer to suggest some information you could include.

We've included some quotes from *Before You Were Mine* (page 98) in this sample answer, but direct quotes from the comparison poem aren't essential; you can use paraphrased examples or summaries to demonstrate your understanding.

LETTERS FROM YORKSHIRE — MAURA DOOLEY

This line is ambiguous. It could refer to the relationship between the two, but it could also suggest that the speaker shouldn't romanticise working outdoors.

Seeing the birds prompts the gardener to write to the speaker. This suggests that their relationship is tied to nature.

The image of the gardener "planting potatoes" creates a sense of hope and optimism for the future.

This means his knuckles hurt from being very cold and heating up suddenly when he comes inside, but the personification of "singing" suggests the man's joy towards writing a letter.

In February, digging his garden, planting potatoes,
he saw the first lapwings return and came
indoors to write to me, his knuckles singing

as they reddened in the warmth.
5   It's not romance, simply how things are.
You out there, in the cold, seeing the seasons

turning, me with my heartful of headlines
feeding words onto a blank screen.
Is your life more real because you dig and sow?

10 You wouldn't say so, breaking ice on a waterbutt,
clearing a path through snow. Still, it's you
who sends me word of that other world

pouring air and light into an envelope. So that
at night, watching the same news in different houses,
15 our souls tap out messages across the icy miles.

Enjambment across stanzas mimics the changing of the seasons.

The sibilance suggests that the speaker is envious that the gardener is so close to nature.

Alliteration and assonance in "word" and "world" reflect how their lives are similar but also different.

This reminds the reader that working outside can be difficult and uncomfortable.

The metaphor suggests the speaker is revitalised by the gardener's letters.

"souls" suggests that their connection is profound and meaningful.

The letters allow the speaker and the gardener to stay connected, despite the distance between them.

Maura Dooley

Maura Dooley (b. 1957) is a British poet who is a Professor of Creative Writing at Goldsmiths University, London. She was born in Cornwall and grew up in Bristol. She spent a few years living in Yorkshire before moving to London. *Letters From Yorkshire* was published in 2002.

> **Comment:** *Letters From Yorkshire* is believed to be about Dooley's relationship with her father.

Maura Dooley

Summary of the poem

The poem describes a man in his garden who notices a bird species returning to the UK. He writes a letter to the speaker to tell her this news. The speaker works in an office, and questions whether the man's life is more "*real*" because he spends time in nature. The speaker enjoys receiving the man's letters because they bring news of nature, and allow her to stay connected to him.

Context and references

Generational differences: The 20th century was a time of enormous change and this impacted British society and family values. Up until the mid-20th century, it was expected that:

- adult children would follow in their parents' footsteps. Men would take over the family business or have a similar profession to their fathers. Women were expected to be homemakers and would focus on raising children and running the household.
- adult children would live close to their parents because there was little reason for them to move away. Employment was often local, and people would marry someone from their hometown.

However, following the Second World War, British society began to change more rapidly.

- Education became more widely available for both men and women. Young adults often left home to attend university, and settled in different parts of the country, sometimes far away from their families.

> **Comment:** Dooley attended the University of York and graduated in 1978.

- Improved access to education meant that more women entered the workforce, and fewer women chose to become housewives.
- The rapid advancement in technology (such as computers and the internet) created new job opportunities, so young adults were less reliant on a family trade to find employment.

> **Comment:** The relationship in *Letters From Yorkshire* reflects some of these generational changes. The poem suggests that the speaker lives far away from her father, and that she works with computers in an office. The speaker's urban office job contrasts with her father's life outdoors. Despite their differences, the two remain close through a shared love of nature.

Themes

Nature
The speaker and the gardener are both interested in the outdoors, and the gardener's letters allow the speaker to stay connected to nature. The speaker reflects whether working outdoors is more meaningful than an office job.

Distance
The speaker and the gardener live far apart, but they keep in touch through their letters.

Family relationships
It is thought that the poem explores Dooley's relationship with her father.

Form and structure

The poem is written in **free verse** and most of the lines are **enjambed**, which closely mimics natural speech. This reinforces the friendly, informal relationship between the speaker and the gardener, and the conversational style of their letters.

Comment: Although the poem doesn't rhyme, the first stanza repeats words ending in '-ing', such as "*digging*", "*planting*", "*lapwings*" and "*singing*". This repetition creates a sense of the gardener's busyness as he works outdoors.

The poem frequently uses **caesura**. This slows the pace, and creates a steady rhythm, which matches the pair's constant presence in each other's lives and the stability in their relationship.

Comment: Each of the five stanzas is made up of three lines. This regular structure could reflect the steady and unchanging nature of their relationship.

The first stanza is written in the third person, and the gardener is referred to as "*he*". This changes in the second stanza to the second person, with the pronoun "*you*". Switching from the third to the second person demonstrates the increasing closeness between the two. In the final line, the speaker refers to "*our souls*". The word "*our*" suggests togetherness, and the connection between the speaker and the gardener.

The first four stanzas convey the distance between the speaker and the gardener by describing their separate lives. This changes in the final stanza, where the pair are described "*watching the same news in different houses*", which highlights their close connection. This gives the poem a satisfying ending as the pair continue their relationship despite the "*icy miles*" between them.

Tone

The poem has an affectionate tone. The speaker and the gardener have a close relationship and send letters to keep each other updated with their lives. The gardener tells the speaker about seemingly insignificant things, such as the lapwings returning, but he knows that she will appreciate the news.

The speaker seems conflicted about her life choices, and debates whether her life is less "*real*" because she doesn't work outside. Although she recognises that working outside can be difficult, she longs for a connection with nature. The speaker is grateful that the gardener can bring her closer to nature through his letters.

The poem has a joyful tone. The gardener enjoys sending letters, as hinted by his "*singing*" knuckles, and the speaker enjoys receiving the letters, as shown by her describing them as "*air and light*".

Language

Representation of the gardener

Hard-working

The gardener is introduced as active and hard-working. He is "*digging*" and "*planting*".

Comment: The gardener's knuckles "*reddened*" when he comes inside. Usually, red is associated with danger, but here, the reddening suggests the warmth and affection between the gardener and the speaker. This is reinforced by his knuckles "*singing*", and this **personification** emphasises the joy he feels writing letters to her.

Uncomplicated

The gardener takes pleasure from simple things, for example, he's so excited by the lapwings returning to the UK that he immediately goes inside to write a letter. This suggests he finds joy in the world around him, rather than material things.

Comment: The returning lapwings suggest that spring is on its way. This gives the poem a sense of hope that warmer weather is round the corner. Birds are often associated with freedom, so the lapwings could represent the gardener's freedom.

The speaker describes the gardener as "*You out there in the cold*". This phrase is made up of simple, **monosyllabic** words which reinforces the simplicity of the gardener's life.

Comment: The gardener is presented positively which reinforces the speaker's affection towards him. If the gardener is Dooley's father, her representation suggests her admiration for him.

Language continued

Natural imagery

The poem begins in "*February*", and references "*ice*" and "*snow*". Usually, cold imagery might reflect a struggling relationship. However, in *Letters From Yorkshire*, the relationship thrives despite the "*icy*" distance between them. This reinforces the warmth and strength of their relationship.

Comment: The enjambment between the second and third stanzas mimics the transition of the seasons.

Importance of communication

The poem explores the importance of communication in a relationship. Despite being separated by "*miles*", their letters allow the pair to remain an important part of each other's lives.

Representation of the relationship

Realistic

Love poetry has a tendency to idealise love, and present it as something extraordinary and overwhelming. In *Letters From Yorkshire*, the affection felt between the pair is presented as realistic and attainable: it thrives despite the everyday reality of their lives

Meaningful

The speaker describes how their "*souls tap out messages*". The word "*souls*" implies that they have a deep and meaningful relationship.

Equal

Their relationship seems equal. Both contribute fairly to the relationship with regular correspondence.

Straightforward

The pair's letters are about simple things, such as the lapwings returning. This suggests that their relationship is uncomplicated.

Language continued

Contrast between rural and urban lifestyles

The speaker contrasts her office job with the gardener's life outside. The speaker describes the gardener's lifestyle as "*that other world*" which suggests it is 'worlds apart' from her own.

The speaker reflects on her lifestyle with the **rhetorical question**, "*Is your life more real because you dig and sow?*". This suggests the speaker is envious of the gardener, and that his life has meaning because he is closer to nature.

Comment: Dooley's generation were amongst the first to work with computers, and the speaker's longing for the outdoors could reflect her feelings towards this shift towards office-based employment.

The speaker describes "*feeding words*" into her computer as part of her job. This contrasts with the gardener who grows "*potatoes*" in his garden. This suggests that the speaker feels her job is less meaningful compared to the gardener who grows real food.

The gardener sees "*the first lapwings return*" whereas the speaker sees a "*blank screen*". This comparison suggests the speaker feels her office job is hollow and unsatisfying compared with the gardener's work outdoors.

The speaker uses **alliteration** in the phrase "*planting potatoes*" which contrasts with the alliteration in the phrase "*heartful of headlines*". The repeated 'h' sound suggests the speaker sighs as she says these words, suggesting her discontent. The word "*heartful*" also suggests the speaker's work takes an emotional toll on her.

The speaker describes the gardener's letters as "*air and light*". This **metaphor** suggests that the speaker feels like she has been outside when she reads his letters, which emphasises how the letters revitalise her and make her feel closer to nature.

Comment: Despite their different lifestyles, the speaker and the gardener watch "*the same news in different houses*". This reminds the reader of the similarities they share.

COMPARING *LETTERS FROM YORKSHIRE*

Here's how *Letters From Yorkshire* could be compared to other poems.

 Remember, you can compare *Letters From Yorkshire* with any poem from the anthology as long as your response is supported with examples. The following examples suggest ways to compare the poems, but they are not complete answers.

Natural imagery

Letters From Yorkshire takes place during winter: it is "*February*", and the gardener is "*breaking ice*" and "*clearing snow*". Usually, winter has negative connotations, as it is associated with lifelessness, however, the natural imagery in *Letters From Yorkshire* creates a hopeful tone. The gardener is described "*planting potatoes*", and this image of new life and growth symbolises hope for the future. Similarly, the gardener sees the "*first lapwings return*". Lapwings are migratory birds, and their arrival suggests that warmer weather is on the way. These images create a sense of optimism which reflects the positive relationship between the speaker and the gardener.

Neutral Tones (see **page 42**) also takes place during "*winter*", but the speaker uses the season to create a pessimistic tone which reflects the struggling relationship between the speaker and his lover. The speaker describes how the "*grey*" "*leaves lay*" on the ground. The colour grey is associated with misery, and the alliteration in "*leaves lay*" reflects how they lie motionless on the ground. This mirrors the lifelessness in the couple's relationship.

Distance

Letters From Yorkshire explores a relationship between a parent and child who are separated by distance but grow closer through letters. The speaker describes how their "*souls tap out messages across the icy miles*". The word "*souls*" suggests that their connection is deep and meaningful, despite the "*icy miles*" that separate them. This is reinforced by the gardener sending the speaker "*word of that other world*". The phrase "*other world*" suggests that their lifestyles are different, but their communication helps them to stay connected.

Mother, Any Distance (see **page 90**) also examines a parent-child relationship affected by distance. However, rather than growing closer, the speaker wants to become more independent from his mother. The speaker is described as "*leaving / up the stairs*" while his mother stays downstairs. This depiction of physical distance represents the son's desire for freedom and independence from his mother. This is reinforced by the tape measure stretched between them reaching "*breaking point*", which represents the son's overwhelming desire to be apart from his mother.

Compare how poets present affectionate relationships in *Letters From Yorkshire* and in **one** other poem from Love and Relationships. [30 marks]

Your answer may include:

AO1 — show understanding of the poems

- Both 'Letters From Yorkshire' and 'Climbing My Grandfather' explore family relationships, and how younger generations attempt to connect with their elders. 'Letters From Yorkshire' is believed to be about Dooley's relationship with her father. The pair stay connected by writing letters, and this brings them closer as the speaker learns about her father's life. 'Climbing My Grandfather' focuses on a grandchild metaphorically climbing his grandfather. As the child climbs, he learns more about his grandfather and their connection deepens.

AO2 — show understanding of the poets' language choices

- Both poems are written in free verse and use enjambment: poetic techniques which more closely match the patterns of natural speech. This informal, conversational style reflects the closeness and intimacy between the speaker and their relative.

- 'Letters From Yorkshire' suggests the pair's growing closeness through the speaker's use of pronouns. Initially, the speaker uses the third person pronouns "his", which suggests a distance between them. However, the speaker then shifts to using the second person, which emphasises their growing connection. In the final line, the speaker uses the plural pronoun "our" which reinforces their connection. On the other hand, in 'Climbing My Grandfather', the speaker only uses the third person to describe his grandfather, which could suggest the distance between them.

- Both poems have a satisfying ending for the reader. In 'Letters From Yorkshire', the speaker describes how their "souls tap out messages across the icy miles". The word "souls" suggests that the pair have a connection on a deep and meaningful level, and the affection they have towards each other is heartfelt and genuine. In 'Climbing My Grandfather', the speaker reaches the "summit" of his grandfather. This suggests that the speaker has achieved his goal, and has gotten to know his grandfather better. Both poems suggest the importance of communication in developing and nurturing family relationships.

AO3 — relate the poems to the context

- The 20th century saw a shift in traditional family relationships. Many children moved further away from their families in search of new opportunities. As a result, some families became less close, and children and grandchildren spent less time with their parents and grandparents. Both poems could be reflecting on the importance of staying connected with relatives by exploring the happiness and joy that family relationships can bring.

This answer should be marked in accordance with the levels-based mark scheme on page 134.

Make sure your answer to this question is in paragraphs and full sentences. Bullet points have been used in this example answer to suggest some information you could include.

We've included some quotes from *Climbing My Grandfather* (**page 122**) in this sample answer, but direct quotes from the comparison poem aren't essential; you can use paraphrased examples or summaries to demonstrate your understanding.

EDEN ROCK — CHARLES CAUSLEY

They are waiting for me **somewhere beyond** **Eden Rock:**
My father, twenty-five, in the same suit
Of Genuine Irish Tweed, his terrier Jack
Still two years old and trembling at his feet.

5   My mother, twenty-three, in a sprigged dress
Drawn at the waist, ribbon in her straw hat,
Has spread the stiff **white** cloth over the grass.
Her hair, the colour of wheat, **takes on the light.**

She pours tea from a Thermos, the milk straight
10 From an old H.P. sauce-bottle, a screw
Of paper for a cork; **slowly** sets out
The same three plates, the tin cups painted blue.

The sky whitens as if lit by three suns.
My mother shades her eyes and looks my way
15 Over the drifted stream. My father spins
A stone along the water. Leisurely,

They beckon to me from the other bank.
I hear them call, "**See where the stream path is!**
Crossing is not as hard as you might think."

20 **I had not thought that it would be like this.**

Annotations:

- The exact location of his parents is undefined, suggesting that the speaker doesn't know where they are, hinting that they are in the afterlife.
- The speaker's parents are young and well-dressed, suggesting that they have been immortalised in heaven at their prime.
- Eden Rock is a fictional place, but "*Eden*" could refer to the Biblical Garden of Eden (a paradise), which hints they are in heaven.
- "*Still*" suggests a moment frozen in time.
- The colour white has heavenly connotations.
- Light is often associated with heaven, and the mother's glowing hair resembles a halo.
- The mother lays out three plates, suggesting that the speaker will join them for the picnic.
- "*slowly*" suggests the scene is calm and peaceful.
- This line creates an almost supernatural image. The three suns could represent the father, mother and the speaker.
- The scene is idyllic: the weather is sunny and the speaker's parents seem relaxed an happy. This suggests that they are content in the afterlife.
- The stream could symbolise a boundary between heaven and Earth. The parents want the speaker to cross the stream and join them in heaven. The phrase "*not as hard as you might think*" implies that death is not something to be feared.
- The final line is separated from the previous stanza, suggesting the physical separation between the speaker and his parents.
- This line is ambiguous: it's not clear what "*it*" refers to. It could mean that the speaker is surprised that this is what heaven looks like.

ClearRevise

Charles Causley

Charles Causley (1917–2003) was a British poet, writer and teacher. He was born in Cornwall, and his poetry is inspired by his Cornish heritage. *Eden Rock* was published in 1988, in the collection *A Field of Vision*.

Charles Causley

Summary of the poem

The speaker describes his parents when they were younger setting up a picnic in the sunshine. The speaker's mother lays out three plates, suggesting that they are waiting for the speaker to join them. The speaker is separated from his parents by a stream, and they encourage him to cross it.

Comment: The poem is a metaphor for Causley's parents waiting for him in heaven. The stream could represent the boundary between heaven and earth.

Context and references

Causley's parents

At the time the poem was written, both Causley's parents had passed away (his father in 1924 and his mother in 1971).

Causley's father was 39 when he died, when Charles was only seven. He died from an injury he sustained during the First World War (1914–18), so Causley's memories of his father's declining health and eventual death may have impacted his early childhood.

Causley's representation of his parents in *Eden Rock* may be influenced by his desire to see them together again, especially when they were both happy, young and healthy.

Comment: Based on the age of his parents in the poem, it is likely that *Eden Rock* is set around 1911, six years before Causley was born. Therefore, the events in the poem are not a real memory from Causley's childhood.

Heaven

Causley was 71 when he wrote *Eden Rock*. He may have been reflecting on his own mortality and what to expect after death. The stereotypical image of heaven consists of angels sat on clouds, however, Causley's depiction of the afterlife is similar to rural England in summer: a grassy field next to a stream on a sunny day. Causley grew up in Cornwall, so he may have drawn on idyllic memories of Cornish summers to create his own interpretation of paradise.

A field in Cornwall by a stream.

Themes

Family relationships
The poem focuses on the speaker reuniting with his parents.

Death
The speaker's parents are deceased, waiting for him in heaven.

Nature
The poem takes place outdoors, in a grassy area by a stream on a warm summer day.

Religion
The title, *Eden Rock*, alludes to the Biblical story of the Garden of Eden, a paradise. The poem explores Causley's depiction of heaven and the afterlife.

Distance
The speaker is physically separated from his parents by a "*stream*". This stream could be interpreted as the boundary between heaven and Earth.

Form and structure

The poem is **semi-autobiographical**: Causley includes elements from real life, but there are fictional elements too (for example, although his parents were real people, the picnic described in the poem probably never happened).

Eden Rock is written in the present tense, which makes the events of the poem seem more immediate. However, the speaker uses the third person in the first four stanzas. This creates a sense of detachment between the speaker and his parents, which reflects how they are separated from him in heaven. The speaker switches to the first person in the final two stanzas, and he interacts with his parents. This suggests that he is close to joining them in heaven.

The poem is made up of six stanzas: the first four stanzas are **quatrains**, the penultimate stanza is a **tercet** (three-line stanza) and the final stanza is a single line. Ending the poem with a single line represents the physical distance between the speaker on Earth and his parents in heaven. The single line could also represent how the speaker feels isolated without his parents.

Comment: The speaker does not cross the stream to join his parents. This could represent how the poet was not yet ready to die.

The poem is largely written in **iambic pentameter** (10 syllables per line, in a pattern of unstressed, followed by stressed). Iambic pentameter closely matches the pattern of natural speech which reinforces the informal and relaxed tone of the poem. This sense of calm is reinforced with **caesura** which slows the pace of the poem.

The poem has an irregular rhyme scheme which uses **half rhymes**, such as "*dress*" and "*grass*"; "*suns*" and "*spins*"; and "*bank*" and "*think*". The half rhymes create an almost dream-like quality which matches the otherworldly content of the poem.

Tone

The poem has an idyllic tone: everything seems perfect. The speaker's parents are young and dressed smartly in their best clothes, the setting is beautiful and the weather is sunny.

Comment: Causley may be projecting his own hopes for his parents in the afterlife. It's human nature to hope that our deceased loved ones are happy and at peace after death.

The poem has a calm tone. The mother moves "*slowly*" and the parents "*Leisurely*" beckon to the speaker. There is no sense of urgency.

Language

Representation of the setting

The poem is set "*somewhere beyond Eden Rock*". "*somewhere*" is imprecise, suggesting that the speaker doesn't know exactly where it is. Similarly, the word "*beyond*" has connotations of heaven, suggesting a place that is just out of reach. Although "*Eden Rock*" isn't a real place, "*Eden*" links the setting to the Biblical Garden of Eden, a paradise.

The couple have their picnic somewhere grassy, beside a "*stream*". This setting may remind the reader of the English countryside, somewhere the poet was very familiar with.

The stream symbolises the boundary between heaven (where the speaker's parents are) and Earth (where the speaker is). The speaker must cross the boundary to be with his parents. The stream is described as "*drifted*", which suggests that it is moving slowly, and the speaker will not struggle to cross it. The speaker's parents say that crossing the stream "*is not as hard as you might think*". The parents offer encouragement to the speaker, implying that dying isn't a painful or unpleasant experience.

Comment: The phrase 'to cross over to the other side' is a euphemism for death. The speaker may have used this phrase as an inspiration for the journey to the afterlife.

The sky is described as whitening "*as if lit by three suns*". The colour white is often associated with heaven, so this may be a deliberate allusion to the heavenly setting. The "*three*" suns could refer to the three family members, but it could also be a Biblical reference to the Holy Trinity: God, Jesus and the Holy Spirit. This reinforces the religious association with heaven.

Language continued

Representation of the picnic

The mother lays out "*three plates*" for the picnic, implying that the speaker will also join them in the afterlife.

The milk is stored in an "*old H.P. sauce bottle*" with "*paper for a cork*". This is a very specific, clear description, which suggests that this may be a memory from the speaker's childhood. This image is also very ordinary and simple: the picnic is relaxed and familiar, rather than elegant and formal.

Representation of the speaker's parents

The parents are in the prime of their youth aged "*twenty-five*" and "*twenty-three*". They are wearing smart clothing, typical of the early 20th century: the father wears a suit made from "*Genuine Irish Tweed*" (a woollen-style fabric, that was originally hand woven) and the mother wears a "*sprigged dress*" (a dress with a floral print). This suggests that Causley wanted to remember his parents at their very best, when they were young and healthy.

The parents are calm and relaxed: the mother moves "*slowly*" and they both beckon "*Leisurely*" to the speaker. They both seem unhurried and untroubled.

> **Comment:** The positive representation of the parents suggest that they are content in heaven. This presents death as something to be welcomed, rather than feared.

The mother's hair is described as "*the colour of wheat, takes on the light*". This creates an image of her hair glowing gold in the sunlight, which may remind readers of a halo, an arc of light around someone's head which symbolises holiness.

Representation of the speaker's relationship with his parents

The parents are eager for their son to join them. They "*beckon*" to him, implying that they are encouraging him to cross the stream, and they reassure him by saying "*it's not as hard you might think*". This suggests that the speaker's parents long to be reunited with him.

> **Comment:** The reader learns very little about the speaker in the poem. It's not clear whether he imagines himself as child, the age he was when he wrote the poem (71) or somewhere in between.

Language continued

Interpretation of the ending

The final line, "*I had not thought that it would be like this*", is ambiguous. It isn't clear what the "*it*" or "*this*" refers to.

One interpretation is that the speaker didn't imagine that this is what the afterlife would look like. Heaven is often represented as white clouds and angels, but this version of life after death is firmly rooted in the speaker's idealised thoughts about his parents, and memories of the British countryside.

Another interpretation is that the speaker didn't realise how easy it would be to accept the process of death and move into the next life. Stereotypical representations of heaven often include a set of gates, guarded by Saint Peter, who only lets the worthy through. The speaker may be implying that you do not need to lead a completely blameless life to be rewarded with a peaceful afterlife.

The speaker may also be surprised that his parents have been immortalised as young, healthy and carefree. Causley's mother was 84 when she died, and his father was 39. Causley may have expected his parents to be the age that they passed away in the afterlife.

COMPARING *EDEN ROCK*

Here's how *Eden Rock* could be compared to other poems.

 Remember, you can compare *Eden Rock* with any poem from the anthology as long as your response is supported with examples. The following examples suggest ways to compare the poems, but they are not complete answers.

Separation

Eden Rock is a semi-autobiographical poem which examines separation. The poet imagines he is separated from his parents by a "*drifting stream*". Although his parents are no longer alive, the speaker presents them in the prime of their life: they are young, happy and healthy, setting up a picnic in a beautiful setting on a summer's day. His parents move "*slowly*" and "*Leisurely*", emphasising how they are calm and untroubled. The speaker's positive representation of his parents in the afterlife reassures him that they are happy which brings him comfort despite their separation.

Walking Away (see **page 58**) is also a semi-autobiographical poem which examines separation between a parent and a child. In *Walking Away*, the separation is caused by a son gaining independence from his father. The speaker is concerned about his son growing up, as he acknowledges that his son will face "*scorching / Ordeals*", a phrase which presents adolescence as painful and difficult. However, like the speaker in *Eden Rock*, the speaker in *Walking Away* also reassures himself about the separation. The speaker acknowledges that "*love is proved in the letting go*", which suggests the speaker sees the separation as a way to prove his love as a parent.

Description of settings

Eden Rock creates a dreamy tone through the description of the setting. The speaker describes a white sky "*as if lit by three suns*". The colour white often has connotations of heaven, and this is reinforced by the reference to "*three suns*", which could allude to the Holy Trinity of Father, Son and Holy Spirit. The speaker's mother and father are setting up a picnic somewhere grassy next to a "*drifted stream*". The slow movement of the stream matches the dreamy, unhurried pace of the poem. The idyllic setting suggests that the speaker's parents are content in heaven, and that the afterlife is not to be feared.

Neutral Tones (see **page 42**) also uses a description of the setting to reflect the tone of the poem. However, unlike the dreamy, happy tone in *Eden Rock*, the mood in *Neutral Tones* is miserable and depressing. Like *Eden Rock*, the sun is also described as "*white*", however, in this poem, this suggests that all colour has been drained from the scene, leaving it dreary and lifeless. This is reinforced by the description of the "*grey*" leaves, which suggests that the leaves are dead. This unpleasant setting creates a gloomy tone, which matches the heartbreak experienced by the speaker.

Compare how poets present separation in *Eden Rock* and in **one** other poem from Love and Relationships. [30 marks]

Your answer may include:

AO1 — show understanding of the poems

- Both 'Eden Rock' and 'Mother, Any Distance' examine separation between parents and children. In 'Eden Rock', this separation is caused by the deaths of the speaker's parents, whereas in 'Mother, Any Distance', the separation is caused by the speaker moving house, away from his mother.

AO2 — show understanding of the poets' language choices

- The speakers are at different stages of their lives and consequently they have different attitudes towards being separated from their parents. Causley wrote 'Eden Rock' aged 71, when both of his parents were dead. Causley's poem has a nostalgic tone, which suggests he longs to be reunited with his parents. However, the speaker in 'Mother, Any Distance' seems much younger, possibly moving into his first home as an adult. He is excited by the prospect of being separated from his mother, as he will gain more freedom and independence.

- Both poems use symbolism to represent separation and connection to parents. In 'Eden Rock', the speaker is physically separated from his parents by a "stream" which could symbolise the boundary between heaven and Earth. However, in 'Mother, Any Distance', the speaker is physically connected to his mother via a tape measure, as she holds the "zero-end", and the speaker unspools the tape measure between them. This symbolises how the pair remain connected despite his desire for physical distance.

- Both poems end with the speakers contemplating their futures. In 'Eden Rock', the speaker considers his own mortality, as he is reassured by his parents that crossing the stream "is not as hard as you might think". This suggests that death is not something to be feared, as it will allow him to be reunited with his parents. In 'Mother, Any Distance', the speaker reaches a window and "an endless sky", which represents the limitless possibilities of the speaker's future.

AO3 — relate the poems to the context

- Both poems explore how our attitudes towards our parents change as we age. 'Mother, Any Distance' reflects how children and young adults often crave freedom from their parents and cannot wait to be independent. However, 'Eden Rock' suggests that once your parents have passed, children will long to be reunited with them.

This answer should be marked in accordance with the levels-based mark scheme on page 134.

Make sure your answer to this question is in paragraphs and full sentences. Bullet points have been used in this example answer to suggest some information you could include.

We've included some quotes from *Mother, Any Distance* (**page 90**) in this sample answer, but direct quotes from the comparison poem aren't essential; you can use paraphrased examples or summaries to demonstrate your understanding.

FOLLOWER — SEAMUS HEANEY

"*globed*" suggests the father's muscles are round and large, implying his strength. This is reinforced with the rounded repeated 'oh' sound in "*shoulders globed*".

My father worked with a horse-plough,
His shoulders **globed** like a full sail strung
Between the shafts and the furrow.
The horse **strained** at his clicking tongue.

Even the horses are straining. This reinforces how difficult the work is.

The speaker admires his father's skill. The caesura emphasises the statement.

5 **An expert.** He would set the wing
And fit the bright steel-pointed sock.
The sod rolled over without breaking.
At the headrig, with a single **pluck**

The repeated 't' sound creates a rhythm, and mimics the sound of the plough slotting into place.

Enjambment mimics the plough turning.

Of reins, the sweating team turned round
10 And back into the land. **His eye**
Narrowed and angled at the ground,
Mapping the furrow exactly.

The father is absorbed in his work which suggests that he is preoccupied by farming, hinting that he doesn't give enough attention to his son.

This emphasises his father's precision.

Unlike his father, the speaker is clumsy and unskilled. This implies that he struggles to live up to his father's abilities.

I stumbled in his **hobnailed wake**,
Fell sometimes on the polished sod;
15 **Sometimes he rode me on his back**
Dipping and rising to his plod.

The speaker literally tries to follow in his father's footsteps. This is also symbolic of the speaker wanting to grow up and be like his father.

Even though the work is strenuous, the father can still carry his son while he works. This shows the father's strength, but symbolises how the father carries the weight of his family.

The phrase 'to be in someone's shadow' means to be 'overlooked because of someone else'. The speaker implies he is unnoticed because of his father.

I wanted to grow up and plough,
To close one eye, stiffen my arm.
All I ever did was follow
20 **In his broad shadow round the farm.**

I was a nuisance, tripping, falling,
Yapping always. **But today**
It is my father who keeps **stumbling**
Behind me, and will not go away.

The caesura marks a time shift. The speaker switches to talking about the present.

The speaker used to follow his father, but now the roles have reversed. The poem's title, *Follower*, could apply to both of them.

Now the father is old, he struggles to walk. This echoes the word "*stumbled*" on line 12, and suggests that the roles have reversed.

The admiration the speaker felt towards his father has been replaced by resentment.

Seamus Heaney

Seamus Heaney (1939–2013) was a poet who grew up in a rural farming community in Ireland. He often drew on his Irish culture in his poetry. *Follower* was published in 1966.

In 1995, Heaney was awarded the Nobel Prize in Literature (a prestigious award that is given to those who have made a significant contribution to their field).

Seamus Heaney

Summary of the poem

A son recalls helping his father plough a field, and admires his father's strength and skill. The son would follow in the furrows made by the plough, but would stumble and fall. Growing up, the son wanted to become a farmer. Now the son is older, the father stumbles after the speaker.

Comment: The title, *Follower*, could refer to either the son or the father. The father follows the horse and plough for most of the poem, and in the final stanza, the father follows his son. Similarly, the title could refer to the son following his father as he ploughs. As a child, the speaker wants to follow in his father's footsteps, admitting, "*I wanted to grow up and plough*".

Context and references

Ploughing

Ploughing describes the action of turning over soil in a field. This is done to bury any weeds and residue from the previous crop, while bringing fresh soil to the surface. Once the field is ploughed, the field is left to dry, and is then planted with seeds.

Today, fields are ploughed using tractors and other machinery, but for many years horses or cows pulled the plough, accompanied by farm workers.

Farmers ploughing a field

Farming

Farms are traditionally handed down through generations of the same family. Children would be taught how to farm from a young age, and would be expected to manage the farm once their parents were unable to continue. For some people, inheriting a farm gives them stability and a clear career path. However, others may feel trapped by the obligation.

Comment: Heaney's father was a farmer, however Heaney decided not to become a farmer, instead he studied English at University and became a teacher. He may have felt mixed emotions towards not taking over the family farm.

GCSE English Literature Poetry Anthology | Love and Relationships

Themes

Family relationships

The poem initially focuses on the speaker's childhood memories of ploughing fields with his father. The final stanza shows how their relationship changes when the son is an adult.

Nature

The poem creates a clear image of working on a farm in the first half of the twentieth century.

Form and structure

The poem is told from the perspective of a son, who recalls memories of his father and his childhood on a farm, so most of the poem is written in the first person in the past tense. However, on line 22, the speaker reflects on his life in the present day, so the tense switches to the present.

The poem is made up of six stanzas, each with four lines. This regular structure could match the steady process of ploughing a field into even furrows. The poem has an ABAB rhyme scheme, but these rhymes are often **half rhymes**, for example "*sock*" and "*pluck*". The use of half rhymes could reinforce how the speaker struggles to live up to his father, or how he feels as though he doesn't belong on the farm.

The speaker uses **caesura** to emphasise important phrases in the poem. For example, the phrase "*An expert.*" ends with a full stop. This causes the reader to pause and reflect on the statement, emphasising the father's skill to the reader.

The use of **enjambment** throughout the poem, specifically between the second and third stanzas, mimics the relentless movement of the plough, and how the farmer and horses repeatedly travel up and down the field.

The first three stanzas focus on the speaker's admiration of his father's skill and strength. The fourth and fifth stanzas focus on the speaker's inadequacies, and how he has struggled to live up to his father. In the final stanza, the speaker describes his father "*stumbling*". This repeats the image of the speaker stumbling in the fourth stanza. Repeating the image of stumbling may remind readers of the circle of life, and how both the young and old rely on others to help them.

Tone

The speaker uses a tone of admiration when describing his father. He focuses on his father's positive characteristics, such as his strength, skill and hard-working nature.

The speaker uses a critical tone to comment on his own failures when he was younger. He reflects that he was a "*nuisance*" on the farm.

The final two lines of the poem convey a tone of resentment. The speaker suggests his father has become a burden who will "*not go away*".

Language

Representation of the father

Strong

The father has "*shoulders globed*". The **assonance** of the long 'oh' sound in the phrase reinforces the rounded nature of his muscles. The word "*globed*" also alludes to the Greek God, Atlas, who was condemned to carry the heavens on his shoulders (often represented by a globe). This suggests that the speaker has a God-like respect for his father because he is responsible for 'carrying the weight' of the family's farm.

Comment: This idea of responsibility for the farm is reinforced by the father carrying his son on his back as he ploughs.

A statue of Atlas

Skilful

The speaker describes his father as "*An expert*" who maps the furrows "*exactly*". This suggests that his father takes pride in his work and implies that traditional farming methods required enormous amounts of skill.

Comment: Most traditional farming methods have been replaced by new technology. The speaker may have wanted to show his respect for the skill involved in his family's occupation and to immortalise a way of life that has largely died out.

Hard-working

The father is described as "*sweating*" suggesting that he works hard. The phrase "*And back to the land*" emphasises his father's pre-occupation with the farm.

Comment: Although the father is represented positively as strong, skilful and hard-working, there isn't any indication of a close relationship with his son, instead, the father seems absorbed in his farm work. The only gesture which could be interpreted as affectionate is when the son is carried on his father's shoulders, but this could be interpreted as the son being a burden on his father.

Frail

The final two lines of the poem imply that the father has become old and frail. He stumbles behind his son, and the son comments that he "*will not go away*". This implies that the father has become a burden, as he is incapable of looking after himself. This represents how parent-child relationships change over time.

Comment: The description of a once strong, powerful man "*stumbling*" is poignant. Many readers will have experienced relatives becoming less capable as they age. Some readers may be critical of the speaker's lack of compassion towards his father.

Language continued

Representation of the speaker

Clumsy

The speaker views himself as clumsy. He "*stumbled*" and "*Fell*", and is described "*tripping, falling*" which implies that he is not suited to life on the farm. The speaker's clumsiness is **juxtaposed** with his father's skill.

> **Comment:** As well as being clumsy, the speaker is described as "*Yapping always*". This suggests he was an irritating, noisy child. This contrasts with the silent presence of his father, whose voice isn't heard in the poem.

Self-critical

The speaker recognises he will never be able to live up to his father. For example, he describes stumbling in his father's "*hob-nailed wake*". This metaphorically suggests that the speaker struggles to live up to his father's expectations. This is reinforced by the speaker's description of being in his father's "*broad shadow*", which suggests he is overlooked.

> **Comment:** The image of the "*broad shadow*" could also suggest that the speaker feels intimidated by his father. The word "*shadow*" has connotations of darkness and negativity, and "*broad*" suggests he finds it difficult to escape his father's presence.

Unrealistic

The speaker seems unsuited to life on the farm, but he still wanted to "*grow up and plough*". This could suggest that the speaker felt that farming was the only occupation available to him, and that he had no choice but to take over the farm one day.

> **Comment:** Although the speaker doesn't seem suited to life on the farm, he has learnt the technical language associated with ploughing, for example, "*shafts*", "*sock*" and "*headrig*". This implies that he learnt a lot growing up on the farm.

Resentful

In the final stanza, the speaker seems annoyed that his father "*will not go away*". This suggests that the father has now become dependent on his son. This resentment contrasts with the speaker's admiration for his father in the opening stanzas.

> **Comment:** Many readers will be able to empathise with this role-reversal, where adult children are expected to care for their elderly parents. Although it's not known whether the speaker has taken over the farm from his father, it seems as though he has accepted a different obligation: the responsibility of looking after his father.

Language continued

Representation of the relationship

Unaffectionate

While the father is established as a hard-working man who provides for his family, he is not presented as affectionate. He is not heard speaking to his son, and there is no evidence that they have a close relationship.

Comment: The speaker describes him as "*father*", rather than 'dad', 'daddy' or 'pa' which suggests they have a more formal relationship.

Strained

Although the speaker seemed to hero-worship his father as a child, this attitude shifts in the final stanza when the speaker reflects on their relationship as an adult. The speaker's lack of compassion towards his elderly father suggests their relationship has broken down.

Comment: Another interpretation of the final two lines of the poem is that the speaker cannot escape the guilt he feels about not working on the farm, and this guilt is symbolised by his father following him wherever he goes.

Representation of nature

Nature is presented in a matter-of-fact way. The speaker doesn't romanticise working outdoors or describe the beauty of nature, instead, the sod is simply there to be "*rolled over*" so that the farmer can plant crops in the field. This reflects the attitudes of farmers who view nature in a practical way.

GCSE English Literature Poetry Anthology | Love and Relationships

COMPARING *FOLLOWER*

Here's how *Follower* could be compared to other poems.

 Remember, you can compare *Follower* with any poem from the anthology as long as your response is supported with examples. The following examples suggest ways to compare the poems, but they are not complete answers.

Admiration towards parents

Follower explores a parent-child relationship that is centred around farming and nature. The speaker admires his father's strength and stamina, describing his father's "*shoulders globed*". The assonance of the long 'oh' sound and the imagery of a globe help the reader to picture the roundness of his father's muscles. This presents the speaker's father as powerful, which reinforces the speaker's respect and admiration for his father's job as a farmer. The speaker is so impressed by his father's abilities, that as a child, he too "*wanted to grow up and plough*", emphasising how parents can influence their children.

Letters From Yorkshire (see **page 66**) also examines a parent-child relationship that is connected to nature. Like *Follower*, the speaker admires her father and respects the manual nature of his work. The speaker uses verbs in the progressive tense such as "*digging*", "*planting*", "*breaking*" and "*clearing*" to convey her father's busyness and hard-working nature. Like the speaker in *Follower*, the speaker in *Letters From Yorkshire* is influenced by her father's work outdoors. She suggests her father's gardening work is "*more real*" than her office job, which implies that she regrets not being able to work outdoors like her father.

Use of half rhymes

The speaker in *Follower* uses an ABAB rhyme scheme, and occasionally uses half rhymes, for example "*plough*" and "*furrow*" in stanza one, "*sock*" and "*pluck*" in stanza two and "*plough*" and "*follow*" in stanza four. These half rhymes contrast with the perfect rhymes, such as "*strung*" and "*tongue*" in stanza one and "*round*" and "*ground*" in stanza three to create a jarring and unpredictable rhyme scheme. The perfect rhymes could reflect how comfortable the father is working on the farm, whereas the imperfect rhymes could suggest that the speaker doesn't feel as though he belongs on the farm.

Eden Rock (see **page 74**) uses half rhymes more consistently than *Follower*, for example "*Rock*" and "*Jack*" in stanza one, "*dress*" and "*grass*" in stanza two and "*suns*" and "*spins*" in stanza three. There is only one example of a pair of perfect rhymes: "*screw*" and "*blue*" in stanza three. Since the majority of the lines are half rhymes or unrhymed, this creates a dreamy, hazy tone, which reflects the dream-like image of his parents in heaven.

Compare how poets present parental relationships in *Follower* and in **one** other poem from Love and Relationships. [30 marks]

Your answer may include:

AO1 — show understanding of the poems

- 'Follower' and 'Singh Song!' examine complicated parental relationships. Both poems are written from the perspective of a son who is expected to carry on the family business. In 'Follower', the speaker is expected to work on his family's farm, whereas in 'Singh Song!', the speaker runs one of his family's shops.

AO2 — show understanding of the poets' language choices

- Both poems explore how the speakers fail to live up to their parents' expectations. In 'Follower', the speaker learns how to plough a field with his father, however, the speaker is presented as being unsuited to farm work. He is described as "tripping, falling", and this contrasts with his father who is described as an "expert". In 'Singh Song!', the speaker has been given the responsibility of running one of his family's shops. However, the speaker neglects his work, and customers complain that it is "di worst Indian shop".

- Although both speakers struggle to fulfil their parents' expectations, the speaker's have different attitudes to their disappointments. In 'Follower', the speaker is self-critical and recognises he was a "nuisance". He also describes being unable to escape his father's "broad shadow", suggesting that no matter how hard he tried, he would never be good enough in his father's eyes. However, in 'Singh Song!', the speaker seems unconcerned by disappointing his family. Instead, he is more pre-occupied with his relationship with his "newly bride", and her presence distracts him from his responsibilities.

- Both speakers show a lack of respect for their parents. In 'Follower', the speaker initially seems to admire his father, however, this changes in the final stanza, where the speaker complains that his father "keeps stumbling / Behind me, and will no go away". This suggests that the speaker is irritated by his father and sees him as a burden. In 'Singh Song!', the speaker allows his wife to disrespect his parents, for example, she swears at his mother, and the speaker doesn't defend his parents, suggesting he does not respect them.

AO3 — relate the poems to the context

- Although the poems were written fifty years apart and were influenced by different cultures (Irish in the case of 'Follower', and Punjabi in the case of 'Singh Song!'), they both explore the expectations that parents can project on to children, and how this pressure can damage parent-child relationships in adulthood. They suggest that relationships between parents and children can be difficult and strained.

This answer should be marked in accordance with the levels-based mark scheme on page 134.

Make sure your answer to this question is in paragraphs and full sentences. Bullet points have been used in this example answer to suggest some information you could include.

We've included some quotes from *Singh Song!* (**page 114**) in this sample answer, but direct quotes from the comparison poem aren't essential; you can use paraphrased examples or summaries to demonstrate your understanding.

MOTHER, ANY DISTANCE — SIMON ARMITAGE

The speaker directly addresses the poem to his mother, which creates a personal tone, but "*Mother*" is a more formal form of address, which suggests distance between the two.

The speaker still needs help from his mother, suggesting that he isn't completely independent.

The speaker uses metaphors to exaggerate the size of the house. This suggests that the speaker sees his new home as unexplored land.

Suggests he is moving away from her emotionally, as well as physically.

Suggests that gaining independence is an adventure.

"*Anchor*" could represent the mother and the stability and security she offers. "*Kite*" could represent the son, and his new-found freedom.

Suggests a turning point in their relationship.

"*pinch*" implies that the mother is holding on tightly, and is reluctant to let go.

Mother, any distance greater than a single span
requires a second pair of hands.
You come to help me measure windows, pelmets, doors,
the acres of the walls, the prairies of the floors.
5   You at the zero-end, me with the spool of tape, recording
length, reporting metres, centimetres back to base, then leaving
up the stairs, the line still feeding out, unreeling
years between us. Anchor. Kite.

I space-walk through the empty bedrooms, climb
10 the ladder to the loft, to breaking point, where something
has to give;
two floors below your fingertips still pinch
the last one-hundredth of an inch ... I reach
towards a hatch that opens on an endless sky
15 to fall or fly.

The speaker isn't sure whether he will be successful, but he needs to be independent to find out.

This could represent limitless possibilities.

? **span** — the distance between a person's thumb and finger when the palm is outstretched
pelmet — a decorative board used to hide a curtain rail

Simon Armitage

Simon Armitage (b. 1963) is an English poet who is the current **Poet Laureate** (see **page 59**). *Mother, Any Distance* is from the collection *Book of Matches*: each poem is short enough to be read in the time it would take a match to burn.

> **Comment:** *Mother, Any Distance* was published in 1993, when Armitage was 30. He may have drawn from his own experiences of reaching adulthood and gaining his independence.

Simon Armitage

Summary of the poem

The speaker is with his mother in his new home. They are using a tape measure to measure for furnishings. The mother holds the tape measure while the speaker moves away from her to the top of the house, unspooling the tape measure between them. The speaker reaches towards a window where he can see the sky.

Context and references

Moving house

Mother, Any Distance focuses on a son moving into a new home. For many children, moving out of their parents' house is the first time they will be physically and financially independent. Although many children look forward to having their own freedom, they will have to pay rent and bills, and learn how to cook and clean up after themselves. This reflects the reality of adulthood: there is more freedom, but also more responsibility.

> **Comment:** Moving out of a parents' house is a rite of passage that most people will experience. This makes the poem relatable, as readers may reflect on their own memories of leaving home.

GCSE English Literature Poetry Anthology | Love and Relationships

Themes

Family relationships

The speaker and his mother work together to measure his new house. This suggests that the speaker still relies on his mother for help.

Distance

The mother holds the end of the tape measure while the speaker moves around the house. This creates physical distance between the pair, which symbolises the speaker's desire for independence.

Form and structure

Mother, Any Distance is told from the perspective of a son and the poem is directly addressed to his mother. This creates a sense of intimacy, as the poem explores their personal relationship.

It is written in the present tense which makes the events of the poem seem more immediate.

The poem is very loosely based on the **sonnet** (see **page 36**) form. Sonnets were typically used for love poetry, so it's an appropriate form for a poem about an affectionate mother-child relationship.

The poem has an irregular rhyme scheme. The first stanza has an AABB rhyme scheme, although the words "*span*" and "*hands*" are **half rhymes**. In the second stanza, lines 6 and 7 are also half rhymes: "*leaving*" and "*unreeling*". In the third stanza, there is an internal rhyme of "*pinch*" and "*inch*", and the poem ends with a **rhyming couplet**. The irregular rhyme scheme could reflect the speaker's apprehension as he gains his independence.

The structure of the poem reflects the changing nature of the relationship between the mother and her son.

First stanza: The speaker needs "*a second pair of hands*". This suggests that he still relies on his mother.

Second stanza: The speaker physically moves away from his mother ("*leaving / up the stairs*") while she still holds the end of tape measure. This reflects how children often desire independence from their parents, but how parents can be reluctant to let go.

Third stanza: In the final stanza, the speaker recognises he needs to be fully independent from his mother, claiming he has reached "*breaking point*". The poem ends with an image of the son reaching towards the sky. This suggests he will embrace his new freedom.

Tone

The poem has a tone of excitement. The speaker is excited about this new chapter in his life and the opportunities that becoming independent will give him.

The poem has a tone of uncertainty, which is expressed by both the mother and the speaker. The mother pinches the end of the tape measure, which suggests she is reluctant to let her son go, and the speaker is uncertain if he will "*fall or fly*".

Language

Representation of the speaker

Close to his mother

The speaker asked his mother to be the "*second pair of hands*" to help measure his new house. This suggests they are close, and the speaker still relies on her.

Comment: However, the speaker calls her "*Mother*" rather than 'mum'. This more formal address hints there could be some distance between the two.

Excited

The speaker seems excited about his new house and the opportunity to live independently. He describes the walls as "*acres*" and the floors as "*prairies*". These **metaphors** compare the house to wide, open spaces, that are ready to be explored, but they hint that the speaker may feel emptiness without his mother.

Comment: This is reinforced by the phrase "*space-walk*" which implies that his new house is an adventure, and a big place to be explored, but it also suggests loneliness and isolation.

Apprehensive

The speaker is nervous about this new chapter in his life. He sees an "*endless sky*", which represents opportunities and possibilities, but he's not sure if he'll "*fall or fly*": he acknowledges that there might be difficulties ahead.

Self-absorbed

The speaker doesn't acknowledge his mother's feelings about him moving out. Although there are hints that she is emotional about him leaving, the son doesn't consider the impact that his actions have on her.

Language continued

Representation of the mother

Reluctant to let go

The mother is described as pinching "*the last one-hundredth of an inch...*" of the tape measure. This implies that she is desperately clinging on to her son, and is reluctant for him to move out.

Reliable

His mother is described as being at "*base*". 'base' can describe 'a starting point for a journey, which often provides safety and provisions'. This suggests the speaker associates his mother with security, and he knows he will always be able to return to her.

The speaker compares unspooling the tape measure to "*unreeling / years*" between them. This suggests that the mother has been a stable part of his life for many years, but the enjambment marks a new phase in their relationship.

Language continued

Symbolism of tethers

The poem uses the image of a son unspooling a tape measure while his mother holds on to the "*zero-end*". This image of two people connected by a line is reinforced by the words "*Anchor. Kite*", and these images symbolise the bond between parents and children, which can be both positive and negative.

Comment: The tape measure could symbolise a timeline of the speaker's life. The mother holding the "*zero-end*" could represent how the mother has been a part of the speaker's life since birth.

Positive

Kites need an anchor to stop them from floating away. Without a weight keeping them in one place, they may get lost or damaged. This represents how parents offer their children stability and keep them safe.

Negative

Anchors keep kites in the same place. The heavy weight stops them from moving about freely. This represents how some children feel frustrated by their lack of freedom and independence.

Comment: The image of a string between the mother and son could also represent an umbilical cord, the link between mother and child in the womb which passes nutrients and oxygen to the baby.

The speaker comments that the tape measure is at "*breaking point*". This suggests that his desire for freedom is overwhelming, but his mother struggles to accept that she must let him go.

Comment: The **enjambment** in the phrase "*where something / has to give*" reinforces how the speaker longs for independence.

COMPARING *MOTHER, ANY DISTANCE*

Here's how *Mother, Any Distance* could be compared to other poems.

 Remember, you can compare *Mother, Any Distance* with any poem from the anthology as long as your response is supported with examples. The following examples suggest ways to compare the poems, but they are not complete answers.

Parental relationships

Mother, Any Distance examines a parent-child relationship, and the poem is told from the perspective of the son as he prepares to move in to a new house. The relationship between the mother and son seems strained as the speaker longs to be independent from her. The speaker admits their relationship is at *"breaking point"*, and he describes his mother using the metaphor *"Anchor"*. Likening his mother to an anchor suggests that he sees her as a hindrance that prevents him from being free.

Before You Were Mine (see **page 98**) also examines a parent-child relationship from the perspective of the child. However, the speaker's relationship with her mother is one of pride, and rather than wanting independence from her mother, the speaker longs to know her mother better. The speaker *"wanted the bold girl winking in Portobello"*, suggesting that she sees her mother as fun and cheeky, and she regrets not knowing her mother in her youth.

Extended metaphors

Mother, Any Distance uses an extended metaphor to represent a growing emotional and physical distance between a parent and child. The speaker describes a tape measure stretched between him and his mother. The mother is stationary at *"base"* whereas the son is *"leaving / up the stairs"*. The description of the mother at *"base"* represents how she offers her son security and stability, and she will always be there if her son needs to return to her.

The speaker in *Sonnet 29 — 'I think of thee!'* (see **page 34**) also uses an extended metaphor to show physical distance in a relationship. The speaker compares her obsessive thoughts about her lover to *"wild"* vines which wrap around a *"palm-tree"*. Comparing her lover to a *"palm-tree"*, suggests he represents stability, and will be a permanent part of her life.

Compare how poets present family relationships in *Mother, Any Distance* and in **one** other poem from Love and Relationships. [30 marks]

Your answer may include:

AO1 — show understanding of the poems

- 'Mother, Any Distance' and 'Walking Away' explore relationships between parents and children who are growing up and gaining their independence. 'Mother, Any Distance' focuses on a son moving into a new house, whereas 'Walking Away' uses the example of a son walking away from a father following a football match. Both poems present the mixed emotions felt by parents and children as they become more self-reliant.

AO2 — show understanding of the poets' language choices

- While both poems explore children becoming independent from their parents, the poems use different perspectives. 'Mother, Any Distance' is written from the perspective of the son, while 'Walking Away' is from the perspective of the parent.

- Both poems show the reluctance experienced by parents as their children become independent. In 'Mother, Any Distance', the mother's fingertips "pinch / the last one-hundredth of an inch" of the tape measure stretched between her and her son. The verb "pinch" suggests the mother is holding on tightly, and is reluctant to let go of the tape measure, and consequently, her son. In 'Walking Away', the speaker using the simile "like a satellite / Wrenched from its orbit" to describe his son leaving. "Wrenched" suggests the parting was painful, and the speaker was reluctant to let his son go. Both poems suggest that children growing up can be a difficult and emotional experience for parents.

- Both poems use imagery of flying to describe feelings towards independence. In 'Mother, Any Distance', the speaker reaches an "endless sky", but is unsure whether he will "fall or fly". This suggests that he is excited by the limitless possibilities his freedom will bring, but he is uncertain whether the next chapter of his life will be positive. Similarly, in 'Walking Away', the speaker compares his son to a "half-fledged thing", suggesting that he is unsure whether his son has the strength to 'fly' and become independent.

AO3 — relate the poems to the context

- Both poems use familiar scenarios to explore a rite of passage for many young people. This makes the poems more relatable to readers and encourages them to explore their own attitudes towards reaching adulthood and becoming independent. Both poems suggest that children becoming more independent can be painful, particularly for the parent.

This answer should be marked in accordance with the levels-based mark scheme on page 134.

Make sure your answer to this question is in paragraphs and full sentences. Bullet points have been used in this example answer to suggest some information you could include.

We've included some quotes from *Walking Away* (**page 58**) in this sample answer, but direct quotes from the comparison poem aren't essential; you can use paraphrased examples or summaries to demonstrate your understanding.

BEFORE YOU WERE MINE — CAROL ANN DUFFY

> The speaker establishes that this recollection occurred ten years before she was born.

> The present tense makes the recollection seem immediate.

> The poem is written in free verse which more closely resembles natural speech, and matches the conversational tone of the poem.

I'm ten years away from the corner you laugh on

with your pals, Maggie McGeeney and Jean Duff.

The three of you bend from the waist, holding

each other, or your knees, and shriek at the pavement.

5   Your polka-dot dress blows round your legs. Marilyn.

> The repeated 'ee' sound mimics the 'hehe' of laughter, and presents her mother as joyful and untroubled.

> "*fizzy*" suggests the mother's sparkle and bubbly excitement.

I'm not here yet. The thought of me doesn't occur

in the ballroom with the thousand eyes, the fizzy, movie tomorrows

the right walk home could bring. I knew you would dance

like that. Before you were mine, your Ma stands at the close

10 with a hiding for the late one. You reckon it's worth it.

> The speaker suggests her mother's life is full of potential. This contrasts with "*the wrong pavement*" on line 17.

The decade ahead of my loud, possessive yell was the best one, eh?

I remember my hands in those high-heeled red shoes, relics,

and now your ghost clatters toward me over George Square

till I see you, clear as scent, under the tree,

15 with its lights, and whose small bites on your neck, sweetheart?

> "*possessive yell*" suggests the speaker was a loud, demanding child, which contrasts with her mother's freedom before the speaker was born.

> The image of her mother is so clear the speaker can smell her perfume.

Cha cha cha! You'd teach me the steps on the way home from Mass,

stamping stars from the wrong pavement. Even then

I wanted the bold girl winking in Portobello, somewhere

in Scotland, before I was born. That glamorous love lasts

20 where you sparkle and waltz and laugh before you were mine.

> This suggests the mother still longs to dance.

> The alliteration mimics the sound of feet hitting the pavement.

> The additional "*and*" in this sentence emphasises what the mother sacrificed when she became a parent.

> The caesura suggests that the speaker's birth was a turning point in her mother's life, and her mother lost her freedom and potential when she became a parent.

Carol Ann Duffy

Carol Ann Duffy (b. 1955) is a Scottish poet and playwright.

Comment: Duffy refers to real places in Scotland in *Before You Were Mine*: "*George Square*" is a civic square in inner-city Glasgow, and "*Portobello*" is a coastal suburb of Edinburgh. This adds to realism of the poem.

She became the first female Poet Laureate (see **page 59**) in 2009. *Before You Were Mine* was published in 1993. The poem is **autobiographical** and examines Duffy's relationship with her mother. Although not mentioned in the poem, Duffy confirmed that the poem is based on her looking at a photograph of her mother in her youth.

Carol Ann Duffy

Summary of the poem

The speaker describes her mother with her friends a decade before she was born and compares her to Marilyn Monroe (see **below**). The speaker imagines her mother going out dancing in her youth, and being told off for staying out late. The speaker acknowledges that her birth ended her mother's carefree life, and she wishes she had known her mother in her youth.

Context and references

1950–60s youth culture

The 1950s and 60s saw the emergence of 'youth culture': young people whose fashion, music tastes, language and values were different to their parents'. An increasing number of young people wanted to rebel against their parents and make their own life choices.

Comment: The speaker's mother is punished by her own mother for staying out late.

In the 1950s and 1960s, young men and women would meet at ballrooms to dance, so many young people knew the steps to popular dances, such as the "*Cha cha cha*" and "*waltz*".

Marilyn Monroe

The poem references this iconic image of the movie star, Marilyn Monroe, who was famous in the 1950s and 60s.

For many people, Marilyn Monroe represented youth, beauty and sex appeal. However, Monroe suffered from mental health issues and died in 1962 from suspected suicide when she was 36.

Marilyn Monroe

Themes

Family relationships

The poem explores a mother-daughter relationship. The speaker acknowledges her mother gave up her "*sparkle*" to raise a child. This reinforces how people make sacrifices when they have children.

Distance

In the first two stanzas, the speaker is "*ten years away*" from her mother. The speaker longs to know her mother when she was younger.

Religion

The speaker and her mother go to "*Mass*", a Catholic service. This contrasts with the "*ballroom*" that her mother went to when she was younger. This reflects how her mother's responsibilities changed when she became a parent.

Form and structure

The speaker is a daughter who directly addresses her mother. Exploring their relationship gives the poem an intimate tone. The speaker's use of **free verse** and **enjambment** closely resemble the patterns of natural speech, which reinforces the conversational style of the poem.

The poem is made up of four stanzas, each with five lines. This regular structure reflects the predictable passage of time.

The poem is structured **chronologically**. It begins "*ten years*" before the speaker was born, and the first two stanzas describe her mother's life as a young adult. The third stanza and the start of the fourth stanza describe the speaker's childhood, and the poem ends with the speaker as an adult reflecting on her mother's youth.

The poem has a **cyclical** structure as it begins and ends with an image of the speaker's mother stood on the "*pavement*". In the first stanza, the mother is laughing with her friends as they "*shriek at the pavement*". This presents her mother as fun-loving and carefree with the rest of her life ahead of her. However, in the final stanza, the speaker's mother teaches her daughter to dance on "*the wrong pavement*", a phrase which suggests that the speaker's mother has made some poor decisions in the past. Contrasting these two images allows the reader to see how parenthood has changed the course of her mother's life.

Tone

The poem has a thoughtful and nostalgic tone. The speaker reflects on her mother's younger years and recognises that her birth ended the freedom of her mother's youth.

The poem has sense of longing. The speaker admires her mother and yearns to know her when she was younger, commenting that she "*wanted the bold girl winking in Portobello*".

Language

Representation of the speaker's mother

Comment: The speaker represents her mother in an overwhelmingly positive way, suggesting the admiration she feels towards her mother.

Carefree

The speaker suggests her mother's youth was carefree. The verb "*shriek*" implies that the women are laughing loudly, and the **assonance** of the 'ee' sound in the words "*three*", "*each*" and "*knees*", mimics their squeals of laughter.

Full of potential

The phrase "*fizzy, movie tomorrows*" suggests excitement, anticipation and glamour, and links back to the description of Marilyn Monroe (see **page 99**). This implies that the speaker's mother had the potential for a 'happy ever after' found in films.

Comment: In the first line of the poem, the speaker's mother stands on a "*corner*". This could foreshadow how her life will soon change direction.

Glamorous

The speaker's mother wears "*high-heeled red shoes*". Red is often associated with passion and glamour, and high heels are a symbol of femininity and sexuality.

Lively

The speaker's mother is described as "*bold*" and "*winking*", suggesting a lively confidence. She is often described dancing, which suggests she is energetic and full of life.

Comment: The speaker's mother teaches her daughter the "*Cha cha cha!*". This hints that motherhood hasn't changed her completely: she's still lively and fun-loving.

Rebellious

The speaker's mother is punished by her own mother for staying out late ("*a hiding for the late one*"). This suggests that the speaker's mother has a rebellious streak. Despite being punished, the speaker's mother thought staying out late was "*worth it*": being punished hasn't deterred her.

Comment: The speaker wasn't alive during her mother's younger years, so it's not clear whether the events of the first two stanzas have been made up by the speaker, or whether they are based on memories that her mother has shared.

Language continued

Representation of motherhood

The speaker suggests that parenthood changed the course of her mother's life by restricting her freedom. When she was younger, the speaker's mother is open to the opportunities "*the right walk home could bring*". This is contrasted with the "*wrong pavement*" in the final stanza, suggesting that becoming a parent limited her mother's potential.

When she becomes a parent, the mother's "*high-heeled red shoes*" become "*relics*", suggesting her glamorous, fun-loving days are behind her. This is reinforced by the idea of the mother's "*ghost*" clattering in heels, suggesting that her carefree lifestyle is dead.

> **Comment:** The speaker seems to blame herself for restricting her mother's freedom.

The mother teaches her daughter the steps to the "*Cha cha cha*". This suggests that the speaker's mother still has a fun and lively side, and she wants to pass on her love for dancing to her daughter.

> **Comment:** The speaker may be criticising how society expects women to lose their individuality once they become mothers, and how their identities are defined by their role as a parent. Society expects mothers to be loving, patient and compassionate. However, the speaker looks beyond her mother's identity as a parent, and focuses on her identity as an individual.

Vibrant language

The speaker uses dynamic, vibrant language to describe her mother, such as "*shriek*", "*fizzy*", "*bold*", "*glamorous*" and "*sparkle*". This reinforces how fun her mother's life was before the speaker was born.

Colloquialisms

The speaker uses informal language like "*pals*" and "*a hiding*" as well as the tag question "*eh?*", which mimics Duffy's Scottish accent. Since the speaker is addressing their mother in the poem, the use of colloquial language creates a personal, intimate tone, and reinforces their close relationship.

Language continued

Representation of the speaker

Possessive

The speaker seems possessive of her mother, which is reflected in the title, *Before You Were Mine*. The word "*Mine*" implies that the speaker feels ownership of her mother. The poem's title is repeated twice in the poem, emphasising the difference in her mother's lifestyle before and after the speaker was born.

Comment: The speaker's possessive language reverses the typical parent-child relationship: usually it is parents who feel 'ownership' towards their children, rather than the other way around.

Jealous

The speaker inserts herself into the poem, reminding the reader (and her mother) of her existence, for example, "*I'm ten years away*", "*I'm not here yet*" and "*The thought of me doesn't occur*". This suggests that the speaker is jealous that her mother had a life before she was born.

The speaker asks, "*whose small bites on your neck, sweetheart?*". This refers to 'love bites' (when someone bruises their partner's skin though kissing, usually on the neck). The word "*sweetheart*" seems parental, as if the speaker is taking on the maternal role. Mentioning love bites makes the speaker seem jealous, suggesting she is envious of whoever is getting close to their mother.

Admiring

As a child, the speaker puts her "*hands in those high-heeled shoes*". This could symbolise how the speaker longs to be like her mother, and walk in her shoes.

Self-aware

The speaker acknowledges that her birth ended her mother's carefree life, and that the decade before the speaker was born was the "*best one*". The speaker seems to regret the impact that she had on her mother's future, and recognises she was a demanding child with her "*loud, possessive yell*".

Comment: Usually, its parents who are presented as restricting their children's freedom. The speaker subverts this stereotype, which shows her self-awareness.

COMPARING *BEFORE YOU WERE MINE*

Here's how *Before You Were Mine* could be compared to other poems.

 Remember, you can compare *Before You Were Mine* with any poem from the anthology as long as your response is supported with examples. The following examples suggest ways to compare the poems, but they are not complete answers.

Self-critical tone

The speaker in *Before You Were Mine* blames herself for restricting her mother's freedom when she became a parent. The speaker presents her mother's youth as fun and carefree, using vibrant language such as "*fizzy*", "*sparkle*" and "*glamorous*" to convey a sense of excitement and unfulfilled potential. Once the speaker is born, her mother becomes a metaphorical "*ghost*", suggesting that her fun-loving days are over. This contrast creates a self-critical tone, as the speaker seems to regret the impact her birth had on her mother's life.

The speaker in *Follower* (see **page 82**) also creates a self-critical tone, and he blames himself for not being well suited to working on his family's farm. The speaker describes himself as "*tripping, falling, / Yapping always*", and the assonance in "*falling*" and "*always*" reinforces his clumsiness. The speaker describes himself as stumbling in father's "*hob-nailed wake*", which emphasises how he blames himself for not being able to live up to his father's expectations.

Colloquial language

Duffy was born and raised in Scotland, and she uses informal, colloquial language in *Before You Were Mine* to create a strong sense of her Scottish identity. For example, she uses the phrase "*a hiding for the late one*" which means 'a beating for the late night', and words such as "*pals*" and "*Ma*" which are typically found in Scottish dialects to mean 'friends' and 'mum'. Since the poem is addressed to the speaker's mother, this informal language reinforces their close relationship and shared Scottish heritage.

Nagra was born in Britain, but his parents emigrated from the Punjab region of India. The speaker in *Singh Song!* (see **pages 114–115**) uses phonetic spellings and non-Standard grammar to reflect his British-Punjabi accent, such as "*di beaches ov di UK in di brightey moon*" as well as references to his Indian heritage in words such as "*chapatti*" and "*sari*". This reinforces the speaker's culture, and emphasises the important role that parents play in shaping their children's identities.

Compare how poets present family relationships in *Before You Were Mine* and in **one** other poem from Love and Relationships.
[30 marks]

Your answer may include:

AO1 — show understanding of the poems
- Both 'Before You Were Mine' and 'Eden Rock' focus on a child's feelings towards their parent(s). Both speakers portray their parents positively, and imagine them in the prime of their lives. In 'Before You Were Mine', the speaker imagines her mother a decade before she was born, as a glamorous, lively young woman. In 'Eden Rock', the speaker immortalises his parents as a happy, healthy young couple in heaven.

AO2 — show understanding of the poets' language choices
- Both speakers imagine their parent(s) at the prime of their life, presenting them as carefree and untroubled. In 'Before You Were Mine', the speaker imagines her mother laughing with her "pals". This presents her mother as full of joy, and the assonance of the long 'ee' sound in the words "McGeeney", "three", "knees" and "shriek" emphasises the 'hehe' sound of laughter. In 'Eden Rock', the speaker imagines his mother "slowly" setting up a picnic, and his father "Leisurely" skimming stones, suggesting they are calm and relaxed.
- Both poems create a tone of longing. In 'Before You were Mine', the speaker yearns for the "bold girl winking in Portobello", wishing that she knew her mother when she was younger. In 'Eden Rock', the speaker longs to be reunited with his parents. He describes how they "beckon" to him, and encourage him to cross the stream, saying "it's not as hard as you might think". This emphasises how the speaker is looking forward to being reunited with his parents once again.

AO3 — relate the poems to the context
- Both poems are semi-autobiographical and draw on a mixture of real memories and fiction. Duffy used a photograph of her mother laughing with her friends as the inspiration of 'Before You Were Mine' alongside her own childhood memories, such as being taught the steps from the Cha cha cha. Causley also uses vivid memories from his own childhood, including the "H.P. Sauce bottle" with a "screw / Of paper for a cork". Using real memories makes the poems seem more heartfelt and genuine, and suggest that children can often feel wistful and nostalgic about relationships with their parents.

This answer should be marked in accordance with the levels-based mark scheme on page 134.

Make sure your answer to this question is in paragraphs and full sentences. Bullet points have been used in this example answer to suggest some information you could include.

We've included some quotes from *Eden Rock* (**page 74**) in this sample answer, but direct quotes from the comparison poem aren't essential; you can use paraphrased examples or summaries to demonstrate your understanding.

WINTER SWANS — OWEN SHEERS

The weather matches the mood of the couple: initially miserable, then hopeful.

The clouds had given their all -
two days of rain and then a break
in which we walked,

The enjambment matches the break in the weather.

the waterlogged earth
5   gulping for breath at our feet
as we skirted the lake, silent and apart,

Turning point (volta) of the poem, which marks a shift in the couple's relationship.

The earth is personified as struggling to breathe and this is reinforced by the repeated 'g' sound in "waterlogged" and "gulping". This could represent how the speaker's relationship is also struggling.

until the swans came and stopped us
with a show of tipping in unison.
As if rolling weights down their bodies to their heads

The swans separate and then reunite. This echoes the couple's relationship.

Caesura creates a pause which emphasises the statement that follows, reinforcing how the relationship is cold and distant.

10 they halved themselves in the dark water,
icebergs of white feather, paused before returning again
like boats righting in rough weather.

The simile suggests that the couple's relationship, like the boats, can survive difficulties.

'They mate for life' you said as they left,
porcelain over the stilling water. I didn't reply

"stilling water" suggests that the water is calming, just like the tensions in the relationship.

15 but as we moved on through the afternoon light,

Light has connotations of hope.

slow-stepping in the lake's shingle and sand,
I noticed our hands, that had, somehow,
swum the distance between us

The internal rhyme of "sand" and "hands" reinforces the connection between the couple.

Sibilance creates a soft sound which mirrors their footsteps in the sand. Shingle and sand can be difficult to walk on, which suggests the couple are prepared to face adversity together.

and folded, one over the other,
20 like a pair of wings settling after flight.

Continues the symbolism of the swans to show the couple's unity.

The poem ends with a couplet, reinforcing the couple's unity. It also has a hopeful tone, suggesting that the couple will reconcile.

Owen Sheers

Owen Sheers (b. 1974) is a Welsh poet. *Winter Swans* is taken from his collection *Skirrid Hill*, which was published in 2005. The collection focuses on themes of separation and divorce.

Comment: 'Skirrid' is derived from the Welsh word 'Ysgyryd' which means 'split' or 'broken'.

Owen Sheers

Summary of the poem

A couple are walking around a lake after several days of bad weather. They are cold and distant towards each other. They notice some swans on the lake, and the unity of the swans causes the couple to show affection towards each other.

Context and references

Swans

The third and fourth stanzas describe the mating ritual of swans. Swans are often used to symbolise love because they mate with the same partner for life.

Comment: The couple are inspired to reunite after watching the swans' affection towards each other.

GCSE English Literature **Poetry Anthology** | Love and Relationships

Themes

Nature
Natural imagery features heavily in the poem, including the weather, the setting of the pond and the motif of the swans.

Romantic love
The poem focuses on a couple whose relationship seems to be strained. However, by the end of the poem there is hope that the couple will reconcile.

Distance
At the start of the poem, the couple are emotionally distant, as they are described as being "*silent and apart*". However, by the end of the poem, the couple appear to have overcome "*the distance*" between them.

Form and structure

The poem is made up of seven stanzas. The first six stanzas each have three lines, and the uneven number of lines could reflect how the couple's relationship is unstable. However, the final stanza is a couplet. This reflects how the couple have reconciled.

The poem is written in **free verse**. The lack of rhyme scheme could represent how the couple are not in unison, and the frequent use of **enjambment** could reflect the emotional distance between them.

The poem is written in the first person, and uses plural pronouns "*we*", "*our*" and "*us*". These pronouns reflect how the speaker still feels connected to his partner despite their relationship struggles.

The events of the poem are structured **chronologically** and unfold over a short period of time. The first two stanzas concentrate on the strained relationship between the couple. The third stanza introduces a turning point with the introduction of the swans, and the third and fourth stanzas focus on the swans' mating ritual. The final three stanzas focus on a small improvement in the couple's relationship, ending with an optimistic tone that gives the reader hope that the couple's relationship will improve.

Tone

The first two stanzas have a strained tone, reflecting the tension between the couple: they seem tense and unhappy, and these emotions are reflected in the rainy weather and "*waterlogged earth / gulping for breath*".

The poem ends with an optimistic tone as the couple hold hands. This affectionate gesture suggests that they will overcome their difficulties.

Language

Representation of the relationship

The couple's relationship changes as the poem progresses.

Uncommunicative

At the start of the poem, the couple "*skirted*" the lake. 'Skirted' can mean 'to walk around the edge of something', but it can also mean 'to avoid talking about something'. This could reflect how the couple aren't talking about the issues in their relationship. This is reinforced by the description of them being "*silent and apart*".

The speaker's partner breaks the silence when she comments on the swans, and how "*They mate for life*". The inclusion of **direct speech** suggests an improvement in the couple's communication.

Comment: However, the speaker "*didn't reply*" to his partner's comment about the swans. This hints that they may continue to have difficulty communicating with each other.

Promising

By the end of the poem, the speaker "*noticed*" that the couple were holding hands. This suggests their hand-holding was a natural reflex rather than deliberate, suggesting that the couple instinctively want to be together.

Comment: The water on the lake is described as "*stilling*". This could reflect how the couple's relationship is becoming calmer, just like the water.

Language continued

Natural imagery

Winter Swans contains a lot of natural imagery. This imagery is used to reflect the mood of the couple.

Weather

The poem's title, *Winter Swans*, suggests the events are happening on a winter's day. Winter is often associated with darkness and lifelessness, which could reflect the strained nature of the couple's relationship.

In the first stanza, the speaker describes how there had been "*two days of rain and then a break*". Rain is often used to represent sadness and misery, and this appears to match the mood of the couple.

Comment: The rain could be a **metaphor** for the tears the couple have cried.

However, "*the break*" suggests that it has stopped raining, hinting that better weather might be on its way. This suggests the couple's relationship may also be due some brighter days.

Comment: In the fourth stanza, the speaker uses the **simile** "*like boats righting in rough weather*". This could also reflect the couple's relationship, and how after a difficult period, they are hopeful for smooth sailing.

After the couple see the swans, they walk in the "*afternoon light*". Light has connotations of hope, which creates a sense of optimism for the couple's relationship.

The setting

The couple walk around a lake. The earth is initially described as "*waterlogged*" and "*gulping for breath*". The **consonance** of the guttural 'g' sound mimics the ground gasping for air, which makes the **personification** of the ground seem even more vivid. The saturated earth could reflect how the couple's relationship is at breaking point: neither can take any more misery.

Comment: The description of the "*earth / gulping for breath*" is an example of **pathetic fallacy**, where something not human is given human emotions.

In the sixth stanza, the ground changes to "*shingle and sand*". This suggests that the couple are standing on firmer ground, both literally and emotionally, but their "*slow-stepping*" implies that their relationship is still delicate.

Comment: The **sibilance** across lines 16–17 mimics the footfalls on the soft earth as it shifts beneath them.

Language continued

Natural imagery continued

The swans

The swans are the focal point of the poem, and watching their mating ritual helps the couple to reconcile. The swans symbolise loyalty and unity:

- The swans move in "*unison*", showing how harmonious their relationship is.
- The swans "*halved themselves*", suggesting they are two halves of a whole, which reinforces their unity. Although they separate, they return to one another, establishing their connection.

Comment: The assonance in "*halved*" and "*dark*" create a sense of harmony in line 10.

- The speaker's partner comments that swans "*mate for life*". This reinforces their loyalty and devotion.

Comment: As well as representing unity, the swans also symbolise how the couple can strengthen their relationship. The swans are described as "*rolling weights down their bodies*". This could reflect how the couple need to unburden themselves if they want to remain together.

By the end of the poem, the couple mimic the behaviour of the swans. Their hands "*swum*" towards each other and settle "*like a pair of wings*". The word "*pair*" in this **simile** reflects their unity, and suggests that the swans have encouraged the couple to reconcile.

Comment: Comparing the couple's relationship to the swans suggests that their relationship is natural.

COMPARING *WINTER SWANS*

Here's how *Winter Swans* could be compared to other poems.

 Remember, you can compare *Winter Swans* with any poem from the anthology as long as your response is supported with examples. The following examples suggest ways to compare the poems, but they are not complete answers.

Pathetic fallacy

The speaker in *Winter Swans* uses pathetic fallacy to establish a bleak mood at the start of the poem. The opening line "*The clouds had given their all*" personifies the clouds, and emphasises the sheer volume of rain that has fallen. This is reinforced with the personification of the "*waterlogged earth / gulping for breath*", where the repeated 'g' sound imitates the sound of gasping. The cumulative effect of these techniques creates an image of a dreary, miserable day, which reflects the emotions felt by the couple in the poem, whose relationship is struggling. This creates a pessimistic tone at the start of the poem.

Similarly, the speaker in *Porphyria's Lover* (see **pages 26–27**) also uses pathetic fallacy to set the mood at the start of the poem. The speaker personifies the "*sullen wind*" that "*tore the elm-tops down for spite*". This image of a vindictive, vicious wind establishes a threatening, foreboding atmosphere which foreshadows the speaker's destructive relationship with Porphyria.

Natural imagery

In *Winter Swans*, a couple with a strained relationship are inspired to reconcile by watching a pair of swans. The speaker describes how the swans "*halved themselves… / …before returning again*". This image suggests that the swans are two halves of a whole, and that they are incomplete if they are apart. Using an example of unity and connection from nature also reinforces how the couple's relationship is natural.

Love's Philosophy (see **page 18**) also uses natural imagery to show connection in a relationship. However, the speaker uses this imagery for a different purpose to the speaker in *Winter Swans*. In *Love's Philosophy*, the speaker uses examples of interconnectedness found in nature, such as how "*fountains mingle with the river*" and "*waves clasp one another*" to try to persuade his lover to be physically intimate with him. Similar to the speaker in *Winter Swans*, the speaker in *Love's Philosophy* uses imagery from nature to present their connection as something natural and beautiful.

Compare how poets present ideas about strong feelings in romantic relationships in *Winter Swans* and in **one** other poem from Love and Relationships. [30 marks]

Your answer may include:

AO1 — show understanding of the poems
- Both 'Winter Swans' and 'When We Two Parted' begin by exploring strained romantic relationships. However, the couple in 'Winter Swans' reunite, and the poem ends with a hopeful tone, whereas the couple in 'When We Two Parted' do not reconcile which creates a cynical, pessimistic ending.

AO2 — show understanding of the poets' language choices
- Both speakers use language with unpleasant connotations to describe their strained relationships. In 'Winter Swans', the speaker uses personification in the phrase "waterlogged earth / gulping for breath". This description of the earth struggling and dying, reflects the couple's unhappy relationship. Similarly, the speaker in 'When We Two Parted' uses unpleasant imagery associated with death to represent the end of his relationship. The speaker's lover is described as having a "Pale" and "cold" cheek, which presents her as almost corpse-like, reinforcing how the relationship has died.
- Both poems suggest that the couples' lack of communication is to blame for their difficulties. In 'Winter Swans', the couple are described as "silent and apart". This emphasises the emotional and physical distance that the couple are experiencing and suggests that they struggle to communicate with each other. In 'When We Two Parted', the speaker also acknowledges the couple's lack of communication and the "silence" between them.
- In 'Winter Swans', the couple are able to improve their troubled relationship, and they end the poem holding hands. This gesture symbolises how they are no longer "apart" and have overcome the "distance" they were experiencing at the start of the poem. However, the speaker in 'When We Two Parted' is unable to overcome the difficulties in his relationship. The speaker repeats the phrase "silence and tears" in the second and final line of the poem. This cyclical structure emphasises how he has been unable to move on from the break-up.

AO3 — relate the poems to the context
- Even though the poems were written almost 200 years apart, both couples struggle with communication. This emphasises how poor communication has resulted in strained relationships throughout the centuries.

This answer should be marked in accordance with the levels-based mark scheme on page 134.

Make sure your answer to this question is in paragraphs and full sentences. Bullet points have been used in this example answer to suggest some information you could include.

We've included some quotes from *When We Two Parted* (**page 10**) in this sample answer, but direct quotes from the comparison poem aren't essential; you can use paraphrased examples or summaries to demonstrate your understanding.

SINGH SONG! — DALJIT NAGRA

The speaker is only trusted to run *"just one"* of his father's shops which implies he isn't ready for more responsibility.

Anaphora shows the couple's connection, and the word *"share"* suggests their relationship is equal.

The customers criticise how the speaker runs his shop but he seems unbothered. This suggests that his work is unimportant compared to his new wife.

The alliteration mimics the sound of his wife tapping her foot. Foot tapping can be used as a sign of impatience, hinting that his wife is waiting for him to come back upstairs.

The juxtaposition of *"gun"* and *"teddy"* suggests two sides to the speaker's wife: she can be threatening as well as affectionate.

I run just one ov my daddy's shops
from 9 o'clock to 9 o'clock
and he vunt me not to hav a break
but ven nobody in, I do di lock –
5   cos up di stairs is my newly bride
vee share in chapatti
vee share in di chutney
after vee hav made luv
like vee rowing through Putney –
10 Ven I return vid my pinnie untied
di shoppers always point and cry:
Hey Singh, ver yoo bin?
yor lemons are limes
yor bananas are plantain,
15 *dis dirty little floor need a little bit of mop*
in di worst Indian shop
on di whole Indian road –

Above my head high heel tap di ground
as my vife on di web is playing wid di mouse
20 ven she netting two cat on her Sikh lover site
she book dem for di meat at di cheese ov her price –

my bride
    she effing at my mum
        in all di colours of Punjabi
25   den stumble like a drunk
    making fun at my daddy

my bride
    tiny eyes ov a gun
    and di tummy ov a teddy

The speaker's father makes him work long hours with no breaks. This suggests the father is overbearing, and expects his son to work hard.

Calling her a *"bride"* rather than 'a wife' suggests the speaker's excitement at the relationship.

"*Putney*" sounds like the Punjabi word for wife, and "*rowing*" suggests their lovemaking is lively and energetic.

Italics represents the customers' voices.

The speaker's wife swears at her mother-in-law and laughs at her father. This suggests she isn't very respectful.

The repetition of the phrase *"my bride"* shows the speaker's preoccupation with his new wife.

? **chapatti** — a type of Indian bread **pinnie** — an apron **plantain** — a larger, savory banana
effing — swearing **sari** — a traditional Indian dress **donkey jacket** — a heavy-duty jacket

"Tartan sari" is a mix of Indian and British cultures, suggesting the speaker's wife is a mixture of both influences.

30   my bride
         she hav a **red crew cut**
         and she wear a **Tartan sari**
         a donkey jacket and some pumps
         on di squeak ov di girls dat are pinching all my sweeties –

The speaker's wife has a short, striking Western-style haircut, suggesting that she is rejecting traditional hair styles.

35   Ven I return from **di tickle** ov my bride
         di shoppers always point and cry:
         Hey Singh, ver yoo bin?
         di milk is out ov date
         and **di bread is alvays stale**,
40   di tings yoo hav on offer yoo hav never got in stock
         in di worst Indian shop
         on di whole Indian road –

"tickle" means 'sex'. The speaker's choice of language suggests a playfulness between them.

The speaker continues to neglect his job and the shop seems to be going from bad to worse.

The phrase *"yoo shoppers"* creates an accusatory tone which implies that the reader is one of the customers who gets in the way of the speaker being with his wife.

         Late in di midnight hour
         ven **yoo shoppers** are wrap up quiet
45   ven di precinct is **concrete-cool**
         vee cum down **whispering stairs**
         and sit on my silver stool,
         from behind di chocolate bars
         vee stare past di half-price window signs
50   at di beaches ov di UK in di **brightey moon** –

The speaker uses poetic language to describe the scene, which reinforces his romantic feelings towards his wife.

The beauty of the moon contrasts with the *"chocolate bars"* and *"half-price window signs"* showing how their love has developed despite the everyday realities of their lives.

This is a nightly ritual for the couple which shows their closeness and intimacy.

         from di stool **each night** she say,
            How much do yoo charge for dat moon baby?
         from di stool each night I say,
            Is half di cost ov yoo **baby**,

The couple call each other *"baby"* which shows the closeness and affection in their relationship.

55   from di stool each night she say,
            How much does dat come to baby?

The speaker thinks their love is *"priceless"*.

         from di stool each night I say,
            Is **priceless** baby –

Ending the poem with a punctuation mark which represents a pause rather than a full stop suggests that their relationship is only just beginning.

GCSE English Literature Poetry Anthology | Love and Relationships

Daljit Nagra

Daljit Nagra (b. 1966) is a British poet. His parents, Sikhs from the Punjab region of Indian, emigrated to London in the 1950s. *Singh Song!* is taken from his collection *Look We Have Coming to Dover!* (2007), which explores the themes of multiculturalism.

Daljit Nagra

Summary of the poem

The poem is told from the perspective of a shop manager who is an Indian immigrant (or first-generation immigrant) whose parents own a chain of shops. The speaker is distracted from his duties by his new wife who lives above the shop. Even though the speaker's customers complain, the speaker doesn't care that he is doing a bad job. At the end of the day, the couple sit together and the speaker tells his wife how much she means to him.

Context and references

Sikhism

There are hints that the couple follow Sikhism (a religion from the Punjab region of India) as the wife browses a "*Sikh lover site*", and the surname 'Singh' used in the poem's title is very common amongst Sikhs.

A Sikh couple.

Comment: The title, *Singh Song!*, is a pun on the word 'singsong' which describes a voice which has a repeated rising and falling rhythm. This could refer to the speaker's voice, since Indians with English as their second language often pronounce English words with a singsong quality.

Some Sikhs choose not to cut their hair as they believe that their hair is a gift from God. Even if women choose to trim their hair, many keep it long. This makes the wife's "*crew cut*" (very short, masculine hairstyle) controversial and rebellious.

Themes

Family relationships

There are hints that the couple have a strained relationship with the speaker's family. The speaker's father makes him work 12-hour shifts, which keeps him apart from his wife. The speaker's wife behaves disrespectfully towards her in-laws, but the speaker doesn't seem to mind.

Romantic love

The couple are recently married (the speaker refers to her as his "*newly bride*"). Their relationship is affectionate (he calls her "*baby*") and passionate (the speaker neglects his job to have sex with her).

Distance

The speaker's job keeps him apart from his wife, but he neglects his duties to spend time with her. When he's not with her, the speaker daydreams about his wife.

Form and structure

The poem has an irregular rhyme scheme which mixes perfect rhymes, (such as "*clock*" and "*lock*"), **half rhymes** (such as "*daddy*" and "*teddy*") and unrhymed lines. This creates a lively and unpredictable rhythm.

Comment: The speaker rhymes "*chutney*" and "*Putney*" in the second stanza. This emphasises the humour in these lines, which adds to the light-hearted tone.

The poem is told from the perspective of the speaker, but the reader also hears other voices, such as the customers of the shop and the speaker's bride. These other voices are illustrated using italics.

The poem shares some similarities with song lyrics. Certain lines are repeated, such as "*Hey Singh, ver yoo bin?*" (line 12 and 37), "*in di worst Indian shop / on di whole Indian road*" (lines 16–17, and 41–42) and "*my bride*" (lines 22, 27 and 30). This repetition is similar to how a chorus in a song would be structured, and makes the poem seem upbeat and lively.

Comment: The song-like form of the poem also reinforces the title, *Singh Song!*.

The first two stanzas introduce the speaker, and his love for his new wife. Stanzas three and eight mainly consist of the complaints of the shoppers, which prevent the speaker from being with his wife. Stanzas five, six and seven represent the speaker daydreaming about his wife, suggesting that even when he's not with her, he can't stop thinking about her. The final four stanzas are structured as a question-and-answer **couplets** between the speaker and his wife. This shows the closeness of their relationship.

Comment: The poem ends with a long dash rather than a full stop. This punctuation mark represents a pause, which suggests that the couple's relationship is only just beginning.

Tone

The poem focuses on the joy felt by a couple in love, so it has an optimistic, happy tone.

The poem is light-hearted, and this is reinforced through the speaker's use of comical imagery, e.g. describing the couple's lovemaking *"like rowing through Putney"*.

There is also a sense of rebellion in the poem. The speaker rebels against his parents by closing the shop to be with his wife. The speaker's wife rebels against stereotypical Indian dress by wearing a *"donkey jacket"* over her sari and having a *"crew cut"*.

Language

Non-standard language

The speaker uses non-standard spellings such as *"ov"*, *"di"* and *"ven"* and non-standard grammar, such as *"newly bride"* and *"brightey moon"* to mimic his Punjabi accent and language patterns. This reinforces the speaker's identity and creates a more personal intimate tone.

Comment: The Punjabi influences in the poem also remind the reader how parents help to shape the culture and identity of their children.

Representation of the speaker

Rebellious

The speaker isn't supposed to take breaks, but when there's no one in the shop, he locks the door to be with his wife.

Carefree

The speaker is unbothered by the customers' criticisms: he's more preoccupied with being with his wife.

Irresponsible

The speaker neglects his job. The customers complain about the stock (*"Di milk is out ov date"*) and the condition of the shop (*"dis dirty little floor"*). The customers think that it is *"di worst Indian shop / on di whole Indian road"*.

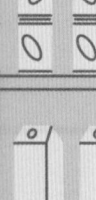

Representation of the speaker's relationship with his parents

The speaker calls his father *"daddy"*. This childish language suggests that the speaker is immature and depends on his family.

The speaker is employed by his father. Although it is typical for small businesses to employ family members, it could also suggest that the speaker might struggle to find a job elsewhere.

The speaker's parents expect their son to work long hours: *"from 9 o'clock to 9 o'clock"*. This suggests that they expect him to prioritise his job.

Comment: The speaker runs *"just one"* of his parents' shops, suggesting that they don't trust him with any more responsibility.

Language continued

Representation of the speaker's wife

Influenced by the West

The speaker's wife seems influenced by Western fashions. She wears Western-style clothes, such as a *"donkey jacket"*, and her sari (a traditional Indian dress) is *"tartan"* (a type of cloth from Scotland). Her hair is styled in a *"red crew cut"* (a very short, masculine cut) which suggests she isn't afraid to look different or rebel against cultural expectations.

> **Comment:** Although the speaker's wife is influenced by the West, she hasn't completely rejected her cultural identity. She and her husband share *"chapatti"* and *"chutney"*: foods typically associated with India, and she still uses her mother tongue when she swears in *"all di colours of Punjabi"*.

Disrespectful

The speaker's wife swears at her mother-in-law (*"effing at my mum"*) and makes fun of her father-in-law. Her husband finds her disrespectful behaviour funny. This suggests the couple have a strained relationship with the speaker's parents.

> **Comment:** In Indian cultures (as with many others) young people are expected to treat elder generations with respect. The wife's disrespect would be shocking.

Representation of the speaker's relationship

Passionate

The speaker cannot wait to have sex with his wife, and he neglects his duties to be with her, showing how much he desires her.

Realistic

The couple's relationship is presented as realistic rather than idealised and unattainable. Each night, they sit in the shop surrounded by *"chocolate bars"* and *"half-price window signs"*: items which aren't usually associated with love poetry. This makes their love seem genuine because it has flourished despite the realities of life, work and family.

Loving

Although they enjoy a sexual relationship, their connection is deeper than physical attraction.

- They *"share"* chapatti and chutney, which reflects the equality in their relationship.
- They call each other *"baby"*, suggesting that their relationship is affectionate.
- In the ninth stanza, the speaker uses eloquent, poetic language when he is with his wife. He describes the *"concrete-cool"* temperature and the *"whispering stairs"* which creates an intimate, romantic tone, reflecting his feelings towards his wife.
- The speaker thinks the couple's love is *"priceless"*, implying that their love is worth more than money.

COMPARING *SINGH SONG!*

Here's how *Singh Song!* could be compared to other poems.

Remember, you can compare *Singh Song!* with any poem from the anthology as long as your response is supported with examples. The following examples suggest ways to compare the poems, but they are not complete answers.

Representation of marriage

Singh Song! presents the relationship of a newly married couple who seem to be deeply in love. The husband neglects his duties at work to spend time with his wife, showing how he prioritises his relationship over his job. The speaker desires his wife, and the lines "*vee hav made luv / like vee rowing through Putney*" suggests they have a passionate sexual relationship. The speaker emphasises the couple's closeness in the final four stanzas of the poem. These stanzas are structured as question-and-answer couplets, which echo the communication and intimacy between the couple.

The Farmer's Bride (see **pages 50–51**) also examines the relationship between a married couple, however, they seem deeply unhappy. Unlike the speaker in *Singh Song!*, the speaker in *The Farmer's Bride* prioritises his work over his relationship, stating: "*more's to do / At harvest-time than bide and woo*". The couple in the poem have been married for "*Three summers*", but it's implied they still haven't consummated their marriage because the wife doesn't want to sleep with her husband. The bride is never heard in the poem, and her voicelessness shows the lack of communication between the pair.

Reality of relationships

The relationship in *Singh Song!* is presented as realistic, rather than idealised and unobtainable. The speaker longs to be with his wife, but everyday life gets in the way. For example, the speaker works long hours as a shopkeeper "*from 9 o'clock to 9 o'clock*" which prevents him from spending time with her. Similarly in the ninth stanza, the speaker describes being with his wife amongst "*chocolate bars*" and "*half-price window signs*", suggesting that his job in the shop is inescapable. Although work gets in the way of their relationship, they value the time they spend together and acknowledge that their love is "*priceless*". This suggests their love is genuine, and it will be able to survive the realities of everyday life.

The relationship in *Winter Swans* (see **page 106**) is also presented as realistic, as it focuses on a couple who are navigating difficulties: something that many couples will experience. The pair are described as "*silent and apart*" which suggests that they struggle to communicate with each other, and that they are drifting apart. However, by the end of the poem, the couple hold hands, and the speaker describes the gesture using the simile, "*like a pair of wings settling after flight*". The word "*settling*" hints that the couple have resolved their difficulties, and the word "*pair*" emphasises their unity. This presents the love in *Winter Swans* as genuine because the couple are prepared to work through relationship difficulties to be together.

Compare how poets present ideas about the power of love in *Singh Song!* and in **one** other poem from Love and Relationships.
[30 marks]

Your answer may include:

AO1 — show understanding of the poems

- Both 'Singh Song!' and 'Letters From Yorkshire' present love as something powerful and positive that can offer a distraction from the realities of everyday life. The couple in 'Singh Song!' are newly married, and their relationship causes the speaker to neglect his job as a shopkeeper. Although the relationship presented in 'Letters From Yorkshire' is "not romance", the letters the pair exchange provide a welcome distraction from the speaker's challenging job and urban lifestyle.

AO2 — show understanding of the poets' language choices

- Both poems suggest that love can transform the mundane into something special. The speaker in 'Singh Song!' sits with his wife behind the shop's counter, surrounded by "chocolate bars" and "half-price window signs", an unromantic and mundane setting. However, the couple look past this to the "brightey moon", which represents how their love has allowed them look beyond the everyday realities of life, and focus on optimism for the future. In 'Letters From Yorkshire', the speaker's friend writes letters about lapwings returning to the UK. Although this message seems ordinary, the speaker comments that her friend's letters are filled with "light and air", suggesting it's not the content of the letters but the affection contained within the letters that revitalise her.

- Both poems suggest that love can distract you from life's realities and difficulties. In 'Singh Song!' the speaker works long hours as a shopkeeper, "from 9 o'clock to 9 o'clock". However, the speaker neglects his job to sneak upstairs to be with his wife. Although his customers complain that he runs the "di worst Indian shop / on di whole Indian road" he doesn't care, because his job is less important than his "priceless" wife. In 'Letters From Yorkshire', the speaker works in an office job with a "blank screen". This suggests that the speaker's job leaves her feeling empty, and the phrase "heartful of headlines" implies that her job takes an emotional toll on her. However, her friend's letters bring "word of that other world", which suggest they provide a welcome distraction from her unfulfilling job.

AO3 — relate the poems to the context

- Although one poem explores romantic love and the other explores a close friendship, both poems reinforce the power of love and the positive impact it can have one someone's life.

This answer should be marked in accordance with the levels-based mark scheme on page 134.

⭐ Make sure your answer to this question is in paragraphs and full sentences. Bullet points have been used in this example answer to suggest some information you could include.

We've included some quotes from *Letters From Yorkshire* (**page 66**) in this sample answer, but direct quotes from the comparison poem aren't essential; you can use paraphrased examples or summaries to demonstrate your understanding.

GCSE English Literature Poetry Anthology | Love and Relationships

CLIMBING MY GRANDFATHER — ANDREW WATERHOUSE

I decide to do it free, without a rope or net.
First, the old brogues, dusty and cracked;
an easy scramble onto his trousers,
pushing into the weave, trying to get a grip.
5 By the overhanging shirt I change
direction, traverse along his belt
to an earth-stained hand. The nails
are splintered and give good purchase,
the skin of his finger is smooth and thick
10 like warm ice. On his arm I discover
the glassy ridge of a scar, place my feet
gently in the old stitches and move on.
At his still firm shoulder, I rest for a while
in the shade, not looking down,
15 for climbing has its dangers, then pull
myself up the loose skin of his neck
to a smiling mouth to drink among teeth.
Refreshed, I cross the screed cheek,
to stare into his brown eyes, watch a pupil
20 slowly open and close. Then up over
the forehead, the wrinkles well-spaced
and easy, to his thick hair (soft and white
at this altitude), reaching for the summit,
where gasping for breath I can only lie
25 watching clouds and birds circle,
feeling his heat, knowing
the slow pulse of his good heart.

screed — 'scree' refers to loose rocks, so "*screed*" could suggest that the skin has a craggy, uneven texture.

Annotations

- **"without a rope or net"**: This phrase suggests risk, but that the speaker feels confident he will be safe.
- **"climbing" metaphor**: The speaker describes metaphorically 'climbing' his grandfather from the shoes up. This metaphor reminds the reader how children often see adults as large, and sometimes challenging to understand.
- **"trying to get a grip"**: This could suggest he's trying to understand his grandfather better.
- **"warm ice"**: The oxymoron "warm ice" introduces a contradiction. The grandfather's skin may feel cool, but the speaker knows that his grandfather is warm-hearted.
- **"earth-stained hand" and "splintered" nails**: suggests that the grandfather is used to tough, outdoor labour.
- **"gently"**: suggests that the speaker is treating his grandfather with care and respect.
- **"firm shoulder"**: suggests that the grandfather is dependable.
- **"loose skin of his neck"**: This unflattering description could reflect how children often don't filter their language.
- **"watch a pupil"**: This suggests that the grandfather is watchful and observant.
- **"soft and white"**: The speaker alludes to the "soft and white" hair being like snow or clouds, which are found at high altitudes.
- **Ending**: The speaker is exhausted when he reaches the top, but the image of clouds and birds suggest freedom.
- **"the slow pulse of his good heart"**: The rhythm of the monosyllabic words reflect the grandfather's heartbeat.
- The poem has a happy ending which reinforces the affection between grandfather and speaker.

Andrew Waterhouse

Andrew Waterhouse (1958–2001) was a British poet who had a keen interest in conservationism and the environment. He earned a Masters in Environmental Science. *Climbing My Grandfather* was published in 2000.

Andrew Waterhouse

Summary of the poem

The poem centres around the speaker metaphorically climbing his grandfather, starting at his shoes and describing the journey up to the top of his grandfather's head.

Comment: The poem could be semi-autobiographical and based on the poet's childhood memories of spending time with his grandfather. While the speaker could be interpreted as literally climbing his grandfather, the poem could also be a metaphor for the speaker getting to know his grandfather.

Context and references

Mountaineering

Comment: A lot of Waterhouse's work draws inspiration from the environment.

A mountaineer at a summit

The speaker compares climbing up his grandfather to climbing up a mountain. Mountaineering can be a dangerous sport: poor weather and difficult terrain can lead to accidents, and it can be difficult for climbers to get help if they are trapped in a hard-to-reach area.

Comment: The poem uses language from the semantic field of mountaineering, including "*traverse*", "*ridge*" and "*altitude*". See **page 125** for more.

Relationships with the elderly

The poem focuses on the relationship between a grandchild and his grandfather, and it may encourage readers to consider their own relationships with elderly relatives. Often, younger generations take their grandparents for granted, and do not know much about them, especially their lives before they became grandparents. The poem could be suggesting the importance of getting to know your elderly relatives while you still can.

GCSE English Literature Poetry Anthology | Love and Relationships

Themes

Family relationships

The poem focuses on a grandson climbing up his grandfather, and the affectionate relationship shared between them.

Nature

The poem uses an extended metaphor to compare the speaker's grandfather to a mountain. This comparison emphasizes the grandfather's age, relative size to the speaker and the excitement the child feels towards 'exploring' his grandfather.

Form and structure

Climbing My Grandfather is told from the perspective of a grandchild. It written in the first-person present tense which makes the poem seem more immediate and exciting for the reader, as if they're watching the climb unfold first-hand.

Comment: The speaker uses the third person to refer to his grandfather using "*his*" (rather than "*your*"). This creates a sense of distance between the speaker and his grandfather.

The poem is written in **free verse**, and this uncomplicated structure could reflect the simple, unsophisticated language patterns that a child would use.

The poem is structured as one stanza, which creates a sold block of text. This could visually represent the size of the 'mountain' and the challenge of the climb. The use of **enjambment** mimics how the speaker is continually climbing.

Comment: The use of enjambment also more closely matches the patterns of natural speech, which reflects how the speaker is recalling a childhood memory.

The structure follows the speaker as he climbs from the bottom of his grandfather to the top. The climb starts "*easy*" and gets increasingly more difficult, matching the reality of climbing an actual mountain. The poem ends with the speaker reaching the "*summit*". This is a satisfying ending for the reader as the speaker has achieved his goal.

Tone

The poem has a tone of curiosity, which reinforces the child-like wonder of the speaker and his desire to learn more about his grandfather.

The poem has an affectionate tone. The grandfather's "*smiling mouth*" suggests his fondness of the speaker.

Language

Extended metaphor

The poem uses an extended metaphor of a grandchild climbing his grandfather like a mountaineer would climb a mountain. This reminds the reader how children 'make believe' and use their imagination during play.

The grandfather is very passive as the speaker climbs all over him. This reflects how elderly grandparents often don't have the energy or ability to actively play with their grandchildren, but the grandfather's willingness to let the speaker climb on him suggests that he is fond of his grandchild and wants to spend time with him.

The metaphor of a 'mountain' reflects how children often see adults as much larger than they are.

> **Comment:** Likening the grandfather to a mountain reinforces his age, but also how he is a stable and solid part of the speaker's life.

The poem includes language from the **semantic field** of mountaineering, such as "*scramble*", "*traverse*", "*ridge*", "*screed*", "*altitude*" and "*summit*". This makes the child's journey seem more believable, and exciting.

Language of learning

The poem could be a metaphor for a grandchild getting to know his grandfather, as he 'explores' the 'mountain'. The speaker uses language associated with learning which develops over the course of the poem. On line 4, the speaker tries to get "*to get a grip*" on his grandfather. This phrase can mean 'to hold on to something', but it can also mean 'to understand something'. This suggests he is starting to get to know his grandfather. On line 10, the speaker uses the verb "*discover*" which suggests he is learning new things about him. On line 26, the speaker uses the verb "*knowing*", which suggests that he has learnt more about his grandfather.

Language continued

Representation of the speaker

Comment: Although it's assumed that the speaker is a child, the language is more sophisticated than a child would use. This reinforces the idea that the speaker could be an adult reflecting on childhood memories.

Curious

The speaker's decision to climb his grandfather reflects his childlike curiosity to explore the world around him.

Comment: The speaker describes "*trying to get a grip*" as he climbs. This suggests that the speaker is trying to get to know his grandfather.

Accepting

The speaker doesn't judge his grandfather for his "*wrinkles*", "*loose skin*" or "*white*" hair: the child accepts his grandfather as he is.

Comment: Pointing out signs of the grandfather's old age also reflects the unfiltered way that some children speak their mind.

Respectful

The speaker climbs his grandfather "*gently*", showing that he treats him with respect.

Satisfied

When the child reaches the summit, he lies "*watching clouds and birds circle*". After the exertion of climbing, the speaker finds peace in stillness.

Comment: The sky overhead and the birds circling could symbolise freedom and the child's future, full of possibilities.

Language continued

Representation of the grandfather

Tolerant

The grandfather is happy to let the speaker climb all over him, and his "*smiling mouth*" suggests he enjoys the speaker's curiosity.

Mysterious

The grandfather has a "*glassy ridge of a scar*" on his arm, suggesting he received a serious injury in his past. This reminds the reader how he had a life before he became a grandfather.

Hard-working

The grandfather has an "*earth-stained hand*" and "*splintered*" nails. This could suggest that the grandfather had a manual job where he worked with his hands.

Comment: The speaker uses the more formal "*Grandfather*", rather than 'grandpa' or 'granddad'. This could suggest a more distant relationship, or it could suggest the speaker's respect.

Kind

The speaker describes feeling his grandfather's "*heat*". This suggests that he has a warm personality. He also has a "*good heart*" which suggests that the grandfather is a kind person.

Comment: The reader doesn't learn much about the grandfather, and we never hear his voice. This reflects how children are more preoccupied with their own lives, rather than finding out about others.

Representation of the relationship

The speaker decides to climb "*free, without a rope or net*". This suggests that the speaker feels safe around his grandfather, and that he won't come to any harm.

The speaker rests on his grandfather's "*firm shoulder*". This creates a familiar image of a child sat on a relative's shoulder, an affectionate gesture which suggests safety and security.

The speaker also sits in the "*shade*" created by his grandfather. This could represent that the grandfather offers the speaker protection.

Comment: The relationship between the grandchild and his grandfather seems affectionate and caring and would be relatable to many readers.

COMPARING *CLIMBING MY GRANDFATHER*

Here's how *Climbing My Grandfather* could be compared to other poems.

Remember, you can compare *Climbing My Grandfather* with any poem from the anthology as long as your response is supported with examples. The following examples suggest ways to compare the poems, but they are not complete answers.

Use of layout

Climbing My Grandfather is written as a single, unbroken stanza. This layout visually represents the challenge of climbing the 'mountain' as the speaker gets to know his grandfather. The lack of line breaks suggests that it is quite a daunting task. However, the poem concludes with the speaker reaching the "*summit*". This implies that the speaker has connected with his grandfather and has been able to get to know him better, which suggests the pair will continue to have a close and loving relationship.

Eden Rock (see **page 74**) also uses layout to visually represent concepts in the poem. The final stanza is a single line which is separated from the previous stanza. This layout reinforces how the speaker is separated from his parents, with them in heaven and him on the other side of the "*stream*" on Earth. The final line also suggests that the speaker feels isolated without his parents, and emphasises the tone of longing in the poem.

Metaphors

Climbing My Grandfather uses an extended metaphor to present the relationship between a grandchild and grandfather. The speaker compares his grandfather to a mountain, which suggests that the speaker could see his grandfather as a permanent, stable part of his life, and the speaker trusts him, as demonstrated by the speaker's willingness to climb "*free, without a rope or net*", which reinforces how the speaker feels safe around his grandfather.

Mother, Any Distance (see **page 90**) also uses metaphors to describe family relationships. The speaker compares his mother to an "*Anchor*", which suggests that his mother symbolises stability and security. Like the speaker in *Climbing My Grandfather*, the speaker's use of figurative language suggests that he trusts his mother, and she is a dependable presence in his life.

Compare how poets present attitudes towards a family member in *Climbing My Grandfather* and in **one** other poem from Love and Relationships. [30 marks]

Your answer may include:

AO1 — show understanding of the poems

- Both 'Climbing My Grandfather' and 'Follower' explore relationships between family members. 'Climbing My Grandfather' uses an extended metaphor of the speaker climbing his grandfather to represent how he is discovering and learning more about his grandfather. 'Follower' examines a son's relationship with his father, and how they spend time together ploughing fields on their farm. Both poems suggest the importance of family relationships, and how older relatives offer support and guidance to younger generations.

AO2 — show understanding of the poets' language choices

- Both speakers admire their relatives. In 'Climbing My Grandfather', the speaker recognises that his grandfather is a kind man with the phrase "the slow pulse of his good heart". Someone who has a "good heart" is thought to be generous, moral and compassionate. This is reinforced by the grandfather's "smiling mouth" which suggests his warmth and affection towards the speaker. In 'Follower', the speaker admires his father's skill. He refers to his father as "An expert" and positioning this phrase at the start of a stanza emphasises its importance to the speaker. The speaker admires his father so much that he "wanted to grow up and plough" just like his father.

- Both poems use the image of a child being placed on a relative's shoulders and back. In 'Climbing My Grandfather', the speaker rests on his grandfather's "firm shoulder", and in 'Follower', the speaker "rode" on his father's back. These images symbolise how relatives support and protect younger generations.

- Although the poems have some similarities, their endings are different. 'Climbing My Grandfather' has a satisfying ending, as the speaker reaches the "summit". This suggests that the speaker has achieved his goal, and has learnt more about his grandfather, which ends the poem on a positive note. On the other hand, the speaker in 'Follower', comments that his father is "Behind me, and will not go away". This suggests that his relationship with his father has deteriorated, and the speaker seems unwilling to support his father in his old age. This is an unsatisfying ending, as it implies that the relationship has deteriorated.

AO3 — relate the poems to the context

- Both poems could be semi-autobiographical and draw upon the poets' experiences of family relationships.

This answer should be marked in accordance with the levels-based mark scheme on page 134.

Make sure your answer to this question is in paragraphs and full sentences. Bullet points have been used in this example answer to suggest some information you could include.

We've included some quotes from *Follower* (**page 82**) in this sample answer, but direct quotes from the comparison poem aren't essential; you can use paraphrased examples to demonstrate your understanding.

OVERVIEW OF THEMES

Here's a summary of the themes across the cluster. Use it to help you quickly identify which poems share similar themes.

	Loss and heartbreak	Romantic love	Death	Distance	Religion	Nature	Obsession & control	Family relationships
When We Two Parted	✓	✓	✓	✓				
Love's Philosophy		✓			✓	✓		
Porphyria's Lover		✓	✓		✓		✓	
Sonnet 29 — 'I think of thee!'		✓		✓		✓	✓	
Neutral Tones	✓		✓	✓		✓		
The Farmer's Bride		✓		✓		✓	✓	
Walking Away	✓			✓		✓		✓
Letters From Yorkshire				✓		✓		✓
Eden Rock			✓	✓	✓	✓		✓
Follower						✓		✓
Mother, Any Distance				✓				✓
Before You Were Mine				✓	✓			✓
Winter Swans		✓		✓		✓		
Singh Song!		✓		✓				✓
Climbing My Grandfather						✓		✓

This isn't an exhaustive list of themes. Instead, it's a summary of some of the themes which are shared by two or more poems and are likely to be relevant to the exam question.

EXAMINATION PRACTICE

Instructions and information:
- We have provided three exam-style questions below. In the exam, you will only be given one question.
- For realistic practice, find an unannotated version of the poem specified in the question, either from your anthology or online.
- You should allow around 45 minutes to answer each question.
- Write your answers on a separate sheet of paper using black ink.

1. Compare how poets present ideas about unhappy relationships in *The Farmer's Bride* and **one** other poem from Love and Relationships. [30 marks]

   You can choose any poem from the anthology, but the example answer uses *Neutral Tones* for comparison.

2. Compare how poets present ideas about family relationships in *Before You Were Mine* and **one** other poem from Love and Relationships. [30 marks]

   You can choose any poem from the anthology, but the example answer uses *Climbing My Grandfather* for comparison.

3. Compare how poets present ideas about separation in *When We Two Parted* and **one** other poem from Love and Relationships. [30 marks]

   You can choose any poem from the anthology, but the example answer uses *Walking Away* for comparison.

EXAMINATION PRACTICE ANSWERS

These answers should only be used as a guide. They are not exhaustive, and there are lots of alternative points that could be made. Your answers may also be structured differently. Use the levels-based mark scheme on page 134 to help you self-mark your answers.

1. Both *The Farmer's Bride* and *Neutral Tones* examine unhappy romantic relationships and how this unhappiness can develop into bitterness. In *The Farmer's Bride*, the speaker is miserable and frustrated because his wife ignores him, whereas the speaker in *Neutral Tones* is unhappy following a break-up.

   Firstly, both poems are from the perspective of a male speaker, and both speakers seem to blame their romantic partner for the breakdown of the relationship, even though there are hints that the speakers should also take some accountability. In *The Farmer's Bride*, the speaker says he's "*hardly heard*" his wife speak, and seems to blame her lack of communication for the difficulties in their marriage. However, the farmer prioritised his work over developing a relationship with his wife-to-be, stating "*more's to do / At harvest-time than bide and woo*". This suggests that the farmer had a practical, rather than romantic, approach to marriage and didn't attempt to get to know her. Similarly, the speaker in *Neutral Tones* seems to blame his partner for the breakdown in their relationship, claiming that he has learnt "*keen lessons that love deceives*". The word "*keen*" suggests that these lessons were painful for the speaker, and the generalisation that "*love deceives*" suggests he feels betrayed by her. However, the speaker also compares himself to "*tedious riddles*" suggesting that his former lover grew tired of his complicated personality.

   Secondly, both poems use cold, lifeless imagery to present the speaker's negativity towards romantic relationships. In *The Farmer's Bride*, it is "*Christmas-time*", and the "*black earth*" is covered with "*rime*". The word "*black*" has negative connotations, suggesting the ground is lifeless, and the coldness of the "*rime*" prevents anything from growing. This reinforces how there is no affection in their relationship. Similarly, the memory presented in *Neutral Tones* happens on a "*winter day*" and the ground is described as "*starving*". Personifying the ground as suffering reflects the couple's dying relationship.

   Finally, both poems have a miserable ending which suggest that the speakers cannot escape the unhappiness caused by their relationships. In *The Farmer's Bride*, the speaker is frustrated by his lack of intimacy with his wife. He repeats the word "*her*" five times in the final two lines, suggesting that he cannot stop thinking about her and he is consumed by thoughts of their unhappy relationship. Ending the poem in this way suggests that the speaker will struggle to put the difficulties in their marriage behind him. Furthermore, in *Neutral Tones*, the speaker uses a cyclical structure, recalling the memory of the "*pond*" in both the first and final stanzas of the poem. This structure suggests that the speaker won't be able to move on from the relationship, and the unhappy memories will continue to haunt him.

2. Both *Before You Were Mine* and *Climbing My Grandfather* explore close family relationships, and the importance of getting to know older relatives. *Before You Were Mine* is told from the perspective of a daughter reflecting on her mother's life before and after parenthood. *Climbing My Grandfather* is told from the perspective of a grandchild, as he metaphorically climbs his grandfather.

   Firstly, both speakers admire their relatives. In *Before You Were Mine*, the speaker creates a vivid picture of her mother as a vibrant, joyful woman. She is described laughing with her friends in the first stanza, and dancing in the second. This presents her as energetic and full of life. The speaker in *Climbing My Grandfather* concentrates on his grandfather's kind, compassionate nature. He describes the "*slow pulse of his good heart*", and this monosyllabic phrase reflects the grandfather's heartbeat. The phrase "*good heart*" presents the grandfather as a compassionate, kind person.

   Secondly, both speakers use poetic forms to establish an informal, conversational tone which reflects the relaxed relationship between the family members. *Before You Were Mine* and *Climbing My Grandfather* are both written in free verse and use enjambment to mimic the natural flow of speech. This conversational style makes the emotions expressed in the poems seem more heartfelt.

   Finally, although both poems explore close family relationships, the speakers have different outlooks on their relationships which are reflected in the endings. In *Before You Were Mine*, the speaker criticises herself for ending her mother's freedom when she became a parent. In the second stanza, the speaker suggests her mother has the world at her feet before she became a parent, and "*the right walk home*" could bring "*fizzy, movie tomorrows*", suggesting that her mother's life is full of excitement, potential and the chance for a 'happily ever after'. However, in the final stanza, the speaker's mother walks on the "*wrong pavement*", suggesting her decision to become a parent was a poor decision, which altered the course of her life for the worse. On the other hand, *Climbing My Grandfather* ends on a positive note. The speaker reaches the "*summit*", which suggests that he has succeeded in getting to know his grandfather. This is a satisfying ending for the reader.

3. Both *When We Two Parted* and *Walking Away* focus on the feelings of loss and sadness caused by separation. *When We Two Parted* examines the heartbreak felt following a break-up, whereas *Walking Away* examines the feelings of emptiness felt by a father as his son gains his independence. Although the poems explore different types of relationships, the grief expressed by both speakers is heartfelt, as the poems are believed to be autobiographical. *When We Two Parted* was written by Lord Byron following the end of a romantic relationship with Lady Frances Webster, and *Walking Away* is about Day-Lewis's relationship with his son, Sean.

Firstly, both speakers use figurative language to express their heartache towards separation. In *When We Two Parted*, the speaker uses imagery to compare his lover to a corpse, describing her cheek as "*Pale*" and "*cold*". This language effectively conveys how the relationship has died, and explains why the speaker mourns the loss of the relationship. In *Walking Away*, the speaker uses the simile "*like a satellite / Wrenched from its orbit*" to describe how the son walks away from the speaker. Satellites are far from Earth, so this simile reinforces the distance between the two, and the emptiness and isolation felt by the speaker.

Secondly, both speakers use vivid verbs to describe the pain of separation. In *When We Two Parted*, the speaker uses the verb "*sever*" to describe the end of the relationship. This word has violent connotations, and suggests that their parting was traumatic, and that the end of the relationship was permanent. Similarly, the speaker in *Walking Away* describes how the memory of the separation "*Gnaws*" at his mind. This animalistic verb suggests that the memory frequently troubles the speaker, and he cannot escape it. This emphasises how difficult the separation was for both speakers.

Finally, both speakers suggest that the pain caused by the separation cannot be healed by time. The speaker in *When We Two Parted*, reflects that even "*After long years*" he will still greet his ex-lover "*With silence and tears*". This suggests that their parting has deeply affected the speaker and he will struggle to move on from the relationship. In *Walking Away*, the speaker still thinks about his son growing up, even though "*eighteen years*" have passed. This also reinforces how heart-wrenching their separation was, and how the speaker has been tormented by the memory ever since. This could imply that the speaker feels guilty about sending his son to boarding school, rather than developing a meaningful relationship with his son during his teenage years.

LEVELS-BASED MARK SCHEMES FOR EXTENDED RESPONSE QUESTIONS

Questions that require extended writing use levels. The whole answer will be marked together to determine which level it fits into, and which mark should be awarded within the level.

The descriptors below have been written in simple language to give an indication of the expectations of each level. See the AQA website for the official mark schemes used.

Level	Students' answers tend to include the following...
6 (26–30 marks)	• Critical, exploratory comparison supported with thoughtful and precise references. • Analysis of writer's methods with subject terminology used skilfully. Exploration of effects of writer's methods to create meanings. • Exploration of ideas / perspectives / contextual factors shown by specific, detailed links between context / text / task.
5 (21–25 marks)	• Thoughtful, developed comparison supported with apt references. • Examination of writer's methods with subject terminology used effectively. Examination of effects of writer's methods to create meanings. • Thoughtful consideration of ideas / perspectives / contextual factors shown by examination of detailed links between context / text / task.
4 (16–20 marks)	• Clear comparison supported with effective use of references. • Clear explanation of writer's methods with appropriate use of relevant subject terminology. Understanding of effects of writer's methods to create meanings. • Clear understanding of ideas / perspectives / contextual factors shown by specific links between context / text / task.
3 (11–15 marks)	• Some explained comparison. References used to support a range of relevant comments. • Explained / relevant comments on writer's methods with some relevant use of subject terminology. Identification of effects of writer's methods to create meanings. • Some understanding of implicit ideas / perspectives / contextual factors shown by links between context / text / task.
2 (6–10 marks)	• Supported comparison with some comments on references. • Identification of writer's methods, and some reference to subject terminology. • Some awareness of implicit ideas and contextual factors.
1 (1–5 marks)	• Simple comments relevant to comparison, with some reference to relevant details. • Awareness of the poet making choices, and possible reference to subject terminology. • Simple comment on ideas and contextual factors.
0 marks	Nothing worthy of credit / nothing written.

INDEX

A
alliteration 45, 71
anaphora 22
archaic pronouns 12
Armitage, Simon 91
assessment objectives vi
assonance 22, 46, 85, 101
autobiographical 35, 60, 99

B
Barrett Browning, Elizabeth 35
Before You Were Mine 65, 96, 98–105
Browning, Robert 28, 35
Byron, Lord 11

C
caesura 37, 53, 60, 68, 76, 84
Causley, Charles 75
chronological structure 100, 108
Climbing My Grandfather 40, 64, 73, 122–129
colloquial language 102
consonance 110
couplets 117
courtship 19
cyclical structure 12, 44, 100

D
Day-Lewis, Cecil 59
death 29, 44, 76
declaratives 21
direct speech 109
distance 12, 36, 44, 53, 60, 68, 76, 92, 100, 108, 117
Dooley, Maura 67
dramatic monologue 29, 53
Duffy, Carol Ann 99

E
Eden Rock 74–81, 88, 105, 128
elegy 44
enjambment 20, 37, 53, 68, 84, 95, 100, 108, 124
extended metaphor 38, 96, 125

F
family relationships 60, 68, 76, 84, 92, 100, 117, 124
Follower 48, 82–89, 104, 129
foreshadowing 29
free verse 68, 100, 108, 124

H
half rhymes 76, 84, 92, 117
Hardy, Thomas 43
Heaney, Seamus 83
hyperbole 22

I
iambic pentameter 76
imagery 14, 22, 31, 62, 64, 111

J
juxtaposition 86

L
Letters From Yorkshire 64, 66–73, 88, 121
loss and heartbreak 12, 44, 60
Love's Philosophy 16, 18–25, 41, 112

M
metaphor 14, 71, 93, 110, 128
Mew, Charlotte 52
monosyllabic 69
Mother, Any Distance 72, 81, 90–97, 128

N
Nagra, Daljit 116
Naturalism 43
nature 20, 36, 44, 53, 60, 68, 76, 84, 87, 108, 124
Neutral Tones 17, 24, 42–49, 72, 80
non-standard language 118

O
obsession and control 29, 36, 53
oxymoron 47

P
pathetic fallacy 30, 110, 112
personification 22, 30, 45, 48, 69, 110
Petrarchan sonnet 36
Poet Laureate 59
Porphyria's Lover 26–33, 48, 57, 112

R
religion 19, 20, 29, 76, 100
reputation 11, 19
rhetorical question 14, 20, 21, 71
romantic love 12, 20, 29, 36, 53, 108, 117
Romantic movement 11, 14, 19, 22

S
semantic field 125
semi-autobiographical 76
sensory language 13
Shakespearean sonnet 36
Sheers, Owen 107
Shelley, Percy Bysshe 19
sibilance 39, 45, 110
Sikhism 116
simile 62, 110, 111
Singh Song! 24, 89, 104, 114–121
sonnet 36, 92
Sonnet 29 – 'I think of thee!' 16, 33, 34–41, 56, 96
superlative 46
symbolism 95

T
The Farmer's Bride 25, 50–57, 120

V
volta 36

W
Walking Away 32, 58–65, 80, 97
Waterhouse, Andrew 123
When We Two Parted 10–17, 32, 56, 113
Winter Swans 40, 49, 106–113, 120

Z
zoomorphism 55

ACKNOWLEDGMENTS

The questions in this ClearRevise textbook are the sole responsibility of the authors and have neither been provided nor approved by the examination board.

Every effort has been made to trace and acknowledge ownership of copyright. The publishers will be happy to make any future amendments with copyright owners that it has not been possible to contact. The publisher would like to thank the following companies and individuals who granted permission for the use of their images in this textbook.

Image on page 11 — Lord Byron © Pictures Now / Alamy Stock Photo
Image on page 11 — The Cheated Wife, 1830–1831 © Heritage Image Partnership Ltd / Alamy Stock Photo
Image on page 19 — Percy Bysshe Shelley © GRANGER - Historical Picture Archive / Alamy Stock Photo
Image on page 19 — Glindoni, Flirtation © Photo 12 / Alamy Stock Photo
Image on page 28 — Robert Browning © Classic Image / Alamy Stock Photo
Image on page 35 — Elizabeth Barrett Browning © The Granger Collection / Alamy Stock Photo
Image on page 35 — Robert Browning Visits Elizabeth Browning © Painters / Alamy Stock Photo
Image on page 43 — Thomas Hardy © GL Archive / Alamy Stock Photo
Image on page 52 — Charlotte Mew © Pictorial Press Ltd / Alamy Stock Photo
Image on page 59 — Cecil Day-Lewis © Pictorial Press Ltd / Alamy Stock Photo
Image on page 59 — The Boys' Book of Soccer for 1946 © Chronicle / Alamy Stock Photo
Image on page 67 — Maura Dooley photo by Isadora Dooley Hunter reproduced with permission from Bloodaxe Books
Image on page 75 — Charles Causley reproduced with permission from David Higham
Image on page 83 — Seamus Heaney © Associated Press / Alamy Stock Photo
Image on page 83 – Ploughing horses © colin13362 / Shutterstock.com
Image on page 91 — Simon Armitage © PA Images / Alamy Stock Photo
Image on page 99 — Carol Ann Duffy © GL Portrait / Alamy Stock Photo
Image on page 99 — Marilyn Monroe © Ian Dagnall Computing / Alamy Stock Photo
Image on page 107 — Owen Sheers © GL Portrait / Alamy Stock Photo
Image on page 116 — Daljit Nagra © Roger Parkes / Alamy Stock Photo
Image on page 116 — Sikh (Punjabi) bride and groom © Matt Hahnewald Photography / Alamy Stock Photo
Image on page 123 — Andrew Waterhouse reproduced with permission from The Rialto.
All other photographs and graphics ©Shutterstock

Walking Away by Cecil Day-Lewis from *Complete Poems*, reproduced by permission of Peters Fraser & Dunlop Ltd.

Letters From Yorkshire by Maura Dooley from *Sound Barrier: Poems 1982-2002* (Bloodaxe Books, 2002).

Eden Rock by Charles Causley from *Collected Poems* published by Macmillan, reproduced by permission of David Higham.

Follower by Seamus Heaney from *Death of a Naturalist*, reproduced by permission of Faber and Faber Ltd.

Mother, Any Distance by Simon Armitage from *Book of Matches* (1993), reproduced by permission of Faber and Faber Ltd.

Before You Were Mine from *Collected Poems* by Carol Ann Duffy. Published by Picador, 2015. Copyright © Carol Ann Duffy. Reproduced by permission of the author c/o Rogers, Coleridge & White Ltd., 20 Powis Mews, London W11 1JN.

Winter Swans from *Skirrid Hill* by Owen Sheers. Published by Seren, 2005. Copyright © Owen Sheers. Reproduced by permission of the author c/o Rogers, Coleridge & White Ltd., 20 Powis Mews, London W11 1JN.

Singh Song! by Daljit Nagra from *Look We Have Coming to Dover!*, reproduced by permission of Faber and Faber Ltd.

Climbing My Grandfather by Andrew Waterhouse appears by permission of The Rialto and the Estate of Andrew Waterhouse.

EXAMINATION TIPS

With your examination practice, use a boundary approximation using the following table. Be aware that the grade boundaries can vary from year to year, so they should be used as a guide only.

Grade	9	8	7	6	5	4	3	2	1
Boundary	88%	79%	71%	61%	52%	43%	31%	21%	10%

1. Read the question carefully. Don't give an answer to a question that you *think* is appearing (or wish was appearing!) rather than the actual question.
2. It's worth jotting down a quick plan to make sure your answer includes sufficient detail and is focused on the question.
3. Start your answer with a brief introduction where you summarise the main points of your response. This can help your answer to stay on-track.
4. Your answer can include the poets' language choices, but also structural choices (such as the ordering of stanzas), themes, and tone.
5. Include details from the poems to support your answer. These details might be quotes, or they can be references to the poems.
6. Examiners tend to award more marks to answers that focus on a smaller number of details in more depth, than a wider variety of points in limited detail. So don't feel pressured to comment on everything in the poems, in fact, concentrating on a few key points can often be more worthwhile.
7. Make sure your handwriting is legible. The examiner can't award you marks if they are unable to read what you've written.
8. The examiner will be impressed if you can correctly use technical terms like 'quatrains', 'metaphor', 'allegory', 'personification' etc, but to get the best marks you need to explore the effect of these techniques.
9. Use linking words and phrases to show you are developing your points or comparing information, for example, "this reinforces", "this shows that" and "on the other hand". This helps to give your answer structure, and makes it easier for the examiner to award you marks.
10. If you need extra paper, make sure you clearly signal that your answer is continued elsewhere. Remember that longer answers don't necessarily score more highly than shorter, more concise answers.

Good luck!

New titles coming soon!

Revision, re-imagined

These guides are everything you need to ace your exams and beam with pride. Each topic is laid out in a beautifully illustrated format that is clear, approachable and as concise and simple as possible.

They have been expertly compiled and edited by subject specialists, highly experienced examiners, industry professionals and a good dollop of scientific research into what makes revision most effective. Past examination questions are essential to good preparation, improving understanding and confidence.

- Hundreds of marks worth of examination style questions
- Answers provided for all questions within the books
- Illustrated topics to improve memory and recall
- Specification references for every topic
- Examination tips and techniques
- Free Python solutions pack (CS Only)

Absolute clarity is the aim.

Explore the series and add to your collection at **www.ClearRevise.com**

Available from all good book shops

  @pgonlinepub

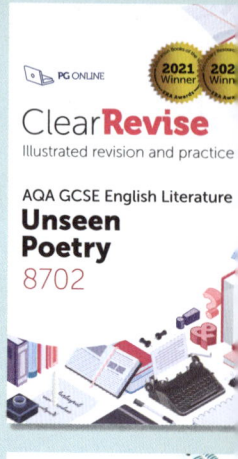
ClearRevise — AQA GCSE English Literature **Unseen Poetry** 8702

ClearRevise — AQA GCSE **Physical Education** 8582

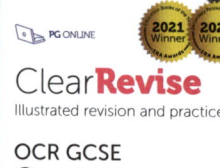

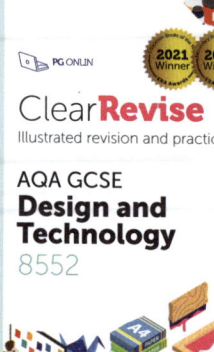

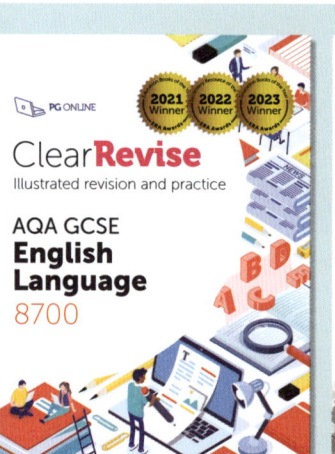
ClearRevise — AQA GCSE **English Language** 8700

ClearRevise — Edexcel GCSE **History 1HI0** — Weimar and Nazi Germany, 1918–39 Paper 3

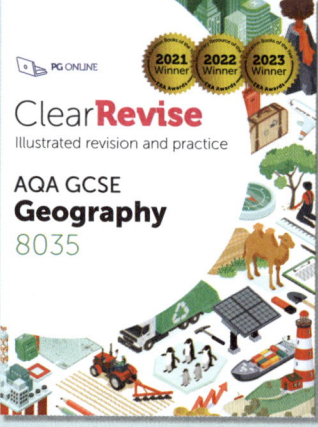
ClearRevise — AQA GCSE **Geography** 8035

ClearRevise — OCR GCSE **Computer Science** J277

ClearRevise — AQA GCSE English Literature **Macbeth** By William Shakespeare 8702

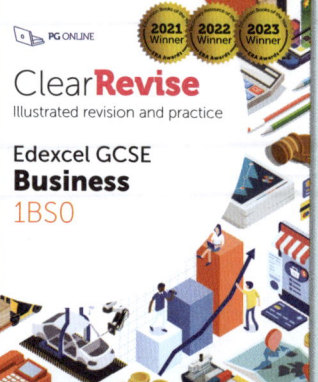
ClearRevise — Edexcel GCSE **Business** 1BS0

ClearRevise — AQA GCSE **Combined Science** Trilogy 8464 Foundation & Higher

ClearRevise — AQA GCSE **Design and Technology** 8552